GOING TO UNIVERSITY
The Secrets of Success

Kevin B. Bucknall, BSc(Econ), PhD

Exposure Publishing, UK

This book is a follow-up to one published in 1996 entitled *Studying at University: How to Make a Success of Your Academic Course*, How-To Books, Plymouth, UK. It has been extensively rewritten and updated.

First published in the UK 2007 by Exposure Publishing

Copyright © 2007 Kevin Bucknall, Exposure Publishing, UK and its licensors. All rights reserved. No part of this work may be reproduced or stored in an information retrieval system (other than for purposes of review) without the express permission of the publisher in writing.

ISBN 978-1-84685-660-0

Front cover design by Virginia Smith

Note: the material contained in this book is set out in good faith for general guidance and no liability can be accepted for loss or expense incurred as a result of relying in particular circumstances on statements made in this book. The laws and regulations are complex and liable to change, and readers should check the current position with the relevant authorities before making personal arrangements.

This book is dedicated to you the reader – may you achieve everything you want in life. Although perhaps you should bear in mind the words from the classic horror story, *The Monkey's Paw*, "Be careful what you wish for, you may receive it."

Contents

List of Figures	ix
Preface	xi
1. University, here I come!	1
OK! How can I do well and also enjoy myself?	1
Why do I want to go to university anyway?	2
What's in it for me?	3
Time to join the grown-ups	5
Freedom means choices!	8
Deciding the essentials: housing, transport, food and finance	10
Everyone should make the most of Fresher Week	17
Don't waste your first-year	22
Case studies	22
Discussion points	23
Summary	24
2. Now I'm here, what am I supposed to do?	25
The low-down on higher learning	25
Why am I here? Many philosophers have asked this	27
There'll be some changes made	30
And you think you've got problems?	31
Adjusting – the change of life	33
Whether you're young or old, strengthen that motivation!	39
Case studies	40
Discussion points	41
Summary	42
3. Learning well now means earning more later	43
How do I start?	43
Tips to make your learning easier	43

Remember: a study-buddy or study-group is the magic secret!	48
Getting to grips with the set textbook	50
Extracting information from journals	52
Bet you can improve your reading!	53
There's something out there: or how to make use of resources	55
Case studies	58
Discussion points	59
Summary	60

4. Teaching, now that'll larn you — 61
Lectures – the course starts here	61
Tutorials and seminars: go in and win!	69
No sweat in the workshops and labs	70
Case studies	71
Discussion points	72
Summary	73

5. Information, information: how to organise and use it — 75
Where the heck is it? Filing your notes for easy access	75
I've really got to start that assignment	77
I've got lots of information – now what?	81
Deciding what you think: suddenly it gets tricky!	82
Avoiding plagiarism: do you copy, good buddy?	85
Case studies	86
Discussion points	86
Summary	87

6. Orals are worth more than the paper they're written on — 89
Doing a dry run	90
Coping with nerves – it's cool to hang loose!	91
Showtime! Delivering that paper	94
Learning to speak body language	95
Questions, questions	97
Case studies	97
Discussion points	98
Summary	99

7. Write on baby! Way to go! — 101
Essay tips – a list of things to avoid	102
Essay tips – watch for these when writing essays	107
Tried the above and I still have problems writing	108

You too can be stylish	108
A late assignment is an unhappy assignment	109
If the worst happens and you fail an assignment	111
Case studies	111
Discussion points	112
Summary	114

8. They're going to examine me, but I feel fine — 115

Getting ready for the exam	115
I hate exams but I've got to do them	117
Putting you to the test: other exam formats	120
Cheating may look enticing but is a poor idea	124
Case studies	125
Discussion points	126
Summary	127

9. Developing team skills – the passport to a better job — 129

We're off! Starting the project	131
Stage one: brainstorming the project	132
Stage two: working in small groups	132
Stage three: putting it together and assembling the overall group report	134
Stage four: examining the draft report	135
So what could go wrong with group projects?	135
Case studies	137
Discussion points	138
Summary	139

10. Role-playing and drama queens – presentation matters — 141

Life, the universe and everything: developing more skills that will stand you in good stead	141
Dealing with essentials: the buck starts here	142
Let the talking begin	144
Yes, they're all looking at you!	145
Visual aids – always give them something to focus on	146
Using props	149
More role-playing tips	150
That important question time in role-playing sessions	153
Case studies	154
Discussion points	155
Summary	157

11. End of part one: the homecoming	**159**
The end of your first term	159
Towards the end of your first-year	160
Case studies	165
Discussion points	167
Summary	168
Appendix A. Some useful Internet URLs	**169**
Appendix B. Favourite free computer programs	**171**
Index	**175**

List of Figures

Figure 1. Tips for living cheaply	20
Figure 2. A checklist of questions for the end of each week	29
Figure 3. Some useful abbreviations and symbols	65
Figure 4. The pattern method of note taking	67
Figure 5. How to start an assignment	78
Figure 6. Some preferred non-sexist words	105
Figure 7. Typical marking systems with approximate equivalents	110
Figure 8. What to do if you fail an assignment	113
Figure 9. A checklist for the day before your exam	118
Figure 10. Some good words and phrases to use	152
Figure 11. Some negative phrases with preferred positive substitutes	153

Preface

When I first went to London University, this was the book I desperately needed but no one had written yet. I wanted one that told me what I needed to know – as opposed to what some remote academic felt I ought to be told – and one that would not bore me to my boots. Well, here's that book now! If you are the first in your family ever to go to university it should be particularly helpful because you have no one at home to ask for advice. So you got through admission impossible and now you're off to Uni! Maybe you saw *Animal House* and it all looked great. Good for you!

Life is beautiful, a wonderful journey through a fascinating world, and going to university puts you into a new and absorbing stage. It will however involve some changes on your part. This book will help you to understand what goes on at university, tells you what you are expected to do, and explains how to do it. You will settle down and adapt quickly, learn more easily, get better marks in assignments and develop marketable skills. And, particularly valuable, you will learn how to study more efficiently and in this way leave more time for the kind of things you really enjoy doing.

Many students seem to prefer getting a good degree to getting a good education, although it is doubtful that they know that Mark Twain once defined education as the path from cocky ignorance to miserable uncertainty. The suggestions in this book can help you get that good degree you want. You can use this advice in two possible ways: you can follow it to improve your marks and gain the best degree you possibly can; or you can follow it to minimise the amount of effort needed to get a simple pass, thus leaving you with a lot more time to enjoy yourself. There is a trade-off to be made between more effort along with good results, and a lot of fun along with a poorer degree. Not all those who come first are always the long term winners – after all, it's often the *second* mouse that gets the cheese. On the other hand, if you only shoot for a pass it might involve you ending up in a boring job with little future. Realising this, many students choose somewhere in between and do a reasonable amount of work; but in the end the choice of what you want has to be yours.

The tips here will work for most of the people for most of the time. You should, however, only follow a suggestion if it works for you. Do make sure you give a suggestion a fair trial before you reject it – some of the techniques require practice to be fully effective.

Don't be put off by the amount of advice – it is the result of decades of experience tutoring and lecturing in and outside universities in the UK and Australia. Relax! You are not expected to learn it all by heart. When you have a need, such as writing an assignment, you can look up the appropriate chapter. If you have not yet started at university, a good way to use the book would be to read Chapter One, *University, here I come,* and Chapter Two, *Now I'm here, what am I supposed to do?*, to get an idea of what you will face. Then read Chapters Three to Seven to gain insight into how to do the work expected. Chapter Eight on sitting exams will be needed later in the term, while Chapters Nine and Ten (developing team and role-playing skills) could perhaps wait awhile, as could the final chapter (the end of your first term and first-year). Each chapter has a summary in the form of bullet points on a separate page. You may choose to read these regularly to remind yourself of what you could usefully be doing; or you might decide to sit back and explore the ideas and suggestions at your leisure and that's cool too.

Throughout your time at college, you will find it useful to refer to the book to look up things when you need them – there will be lots of such opportunities! And if you ever contemplate dropping out, the recommendations on motivating yourself might help to keep you at Uni. Currently graduates in the UK earn roughly 25 per cent more than those who leave school at eighteen, as well as having more interesting jobs, lower levels of unemployment and, for some reason, enjoying better health. So it is worth getting that degree if you can.

If you are still attending school, you will find many of the suggestions helpful, especially the chapters on improving your study skills, writing essays, and sitting exams. You also have one major advantage over those already going to college: in life, almost everything you do gets better the more you do it, so that improving your study skills as early as you can gives you a head start.

While you are still at school it is worth doing a few things to make yourself stand out in a university interview: you might join a few local clubs; work on your school newspaper (or start one); or perhaps take up a musical instrument. Looking like an interesting person can make the difference between being accepted or rejected, as the competition for entry is often fierce at a good institution.

For those already at university, this book could become your manual – an easily accessible source of guidance throughout your university life. Dip into it as you feel the need. For those occasions when you are dipping in rather than reading through, I have occasionally repeated a piece of advice useful for that particular section; for example avoiding the shotgun technique appears in Chapter Seven on writing essays and again in Chapter Eight on writing exam papers.

Be aware that the above suggestions on making university applicants look interesting apply to you even more: this time it is for the job interviews to come. An increasing number of people now get a degree so you have to show you are that much better than the pack. And if the person who interviews you also likes your particular sport or hobby, or approves of participation in things like voluntary work or politics, it can help you get the position you want.

In order to make this book more fun and hopefully interesting enough to let you enjoy reading it, I have scattered a few jokes about, usually marked with a little smiley face and in a smaller font. When you are reading the book for the second or third time, or looking up an issue when you need it, these should not distract or detain you – it's easy to ignore them.

The institutional description relates to England but you should be aware that institutions vary from country to country and from time to time. For convenience, the word "term" (three a year, often about ten weeks each) not "semester" (two a year of around 15 weeks) is used throughout.

1. University, here I come!

OK! HOW CAN I DO WELL AND ALSO ENJOY MYSELF?

Life at university is fun, fun, fun – and of course quite a bit of work.

Well done! You have made it to a Uni or college and this is the start of a really great time, now you are out of your school daze. If you have been told that these were the happiest days of your life, you were probably being lied to. University is far better in almost every way: you have freedom, little responsibility, and an interesting set of new friends. I confess I rather envy you your good fortune – still, been there, done that, bought the T-shirt; now it's your turn.

One of the main things you will almost certainly have to do is learn how to learn. You probably assume that you know how to do this but many students have mostly been *taught* by others and have not really had to learn much on their own. From now on you will be doing a lot of learning so you might as well do it efficiently. Think about it! If you study efficiently it leaves you with a lot more time for doing stuff that you really enjoy! Three elements seem to be common to those who do well at university. Firstly, they go to all set lectures, tutorials, seminars, workshops or laboratory sessions, where they pay attention, and take notes. Secondly, they work for long hours on their own, outside the formal class time. Thirdly, they use their time effectively. What makes them work hard is strong motivation. With a determined will to succeed you can achieve almost anything you want in life. Such determination is crucial if you want to do well – think how much you already know about a particular sport or hobby that really interests you. Try to increase your motivation by following the advice below and regularly doing the things suggested.

Determination plus adjustment equals success
A good way to start your adjustment to university life is to think about why you are going and make your own list of reasons. Keep this and read it regularly – reminding yourself of your original reasons can help strengthen your determination to succeed.

WHY DO I WANT TO GO TO UNIVERSITY ANYWAY? SOME POSSIBLE REASONS (BUT MAKE YOUR OWN LIST)

- My parents and family expect me to go.
- My friends are all going so I'm off too.
- I wish to enjoy the life of a student, which sounds (and is) attractive.
- I'm postponing decisions about what to do with my life.
- I am unable to find a job.
- I want qualifications for a particular career I have in mind.
- I wish to learn about something that really interests me.
- I want a job with real power (though power is like a steep cliff: only reptiles and eagles tend to get to the top easily).
- It would be nice to broaden my mind and improve my quality as a human being (OK, it's rare!).
- I'd like to find intellectual stimulation and enjoyment.
- I may be returning to study after some years in the work force because I need a challenge, or can now afford to get an education.
- Like Aristotle, I believe that education is the best provision for old age.
- I was unable to get into Hogwarts College.
- I want to earn decent money once qualified – yes!!!

WHAT'S IN IT FOR ME?

☺   I'm not selfish – I really do deserve more!   ☺

Going to university gives you the opportunity to think creatively, to learn how to organise your thoughts, and then to express them clearly. You can derive three major benefits: knowledge, skills and personal development.

Knowledge
- In its broadest sense, knowledge consists of facts and theories; it helps you break out of your ignobubble.
- But knowledge gets out of date quickly – it matters in the short term for when you are doing exams, but is probably the least important benefit in the long run. Even in practical subjects like medicine and law, facts and theories are subject to change but the other skills remain of value to you for ever.

Learning transferable skills for your whole working life – a prime gain
These are portable skills that go with you, and if you want a good well-paid job you definitely need them. People now tend to switch direction several times during their working life: to climb the ladder of success you need to be lord of the rungs; and onward and upward is the way to go.

The skills you can get include the ability to do the following both quickly and competently:
- Communicate (orally and in writing) effortlessly.
- Manage your time effectively.
- Work in a team successfully.
- Organise information properly.
- Tackle questions and problems sensibly.
- Win people over to your view as you argue persuasively.
- Analyse issues logically and convincingly.
- Prioritise your tasks quickly.

And:
- Make and keep a wide circle of personal friends.
- Develop a network of business contacts.

Developing as a human being – another real gain
- Expanding your mind, engaging in self-discovery and furthering your personal development.
- Building self-discipline and self-confidence.
- Growing up – well, it has to be done sometime.

University is different from school or working in a job

Compared with going to school – it's a lot better!
- There are no teachers to control or bug you.
- There is usually no check-up on whether you attend classes or not.
- There are no parents to force you out of bed in a morning – high noon is possible!
- The freedom is genuine and really great.
- To an extent this can all be alarming as you are now on your own.
- But you will learn below how to cope with and enjoy the new freedom without losing track of your main goal: getting that degree.

☺ When arguing about food, you shouldn't tell a Frenchman that it's a crock monsieur. ☺

Compared with working in a job – it's fantastic!
- There are no set hours.
- There is no boss.
- There is no profit and loss to worry about.
- There are no dress standards.
- There are no office or factory politics to keep you on your defensive toes.
- The freedom can be exhilarating and you now have the time to do stuff you really want.
- But you have no regular pay packet – bummer!

TIME TO JOIN THE GROWN-UPS

☺　　　Sometimes I sits and thinks, and sometimes I just sits.　　　☺

We all grow up as individuals with our own unique set of experiences. Growing up involves uncertainty and worry about the physical and emotional changes which occur; concern about who we are turning into; coping with mood-swings and feelings of insecurity; concern about dealing with relationships; and maybe developing critical views of your parents and the feeling that they do not understand you.

Self-development involves

Taking responsibility for your actions
No longer can you blame others (parents, teachers, or friends) for what you do – you are now responsible for your own behaviour.

Gaining experience
Gaining experience means trying new things, but if any of these involve losing control of rational decision-taking ability, you should either avoid it or be very careful indeed. Experimenting with drugs, for example, can be addictive, cause personality change, or lead to behaviour you might not normally contemplate. Experience is a good teacher but at the price she charges she certainly ought to be.

Facing challenges and tackling them
If you tackle challenges successfully it is excellent, but even a failure can provide a valuable learning experience – you can think about what went wrong, what you might have done to avoid it, and what you can do next time around.

Hard work and persistence
In life, nothing important comes without effort, and you will have to strive hard for what you want. A sensible motto is: "Work, don't shirk!"

Learning about the big world out there

Increasing your experiences
Going to university is a major change in your life and will provide many new experiences, many interesting, some valuable, and a few wonderful.

Learning from others
There is little point in reinventing the wheel. You should take the chance to study and learn from those who have gone before.

> ☺ Smoke bomb = a student who regularly enjoys marijuana – then fails the exams. ☺

Making your own mind up about that knowledge
Not everything you read or are told by others is true, or perhaps not the whole truth. You must think about what you learn and whilst remembering it, question and criticise it. All is not what it appears – *True Lies* was not just the name of a movie.

Shaping up to the new life
Your life at university will consist largely of three elements: studying in a variety of different ways; being involved in clubs or societies; and socialising.

Studying
This is your main aim – you need that degree – so you do not get much benefit from dropping out early or failing. You are about to learn how to learn. Lectures, tutorials, workshops, lab time, sitting around discussing issues until late at night ... there's a lot to do so let's try to enjoy it.

Social life and partying
This is an important and enjoyable area. You need to relax and enjoy your university experience – it is the best time of life for many people. Get in there! But be careful not to overdo it... except maybe in Fresher Week.

Even mathematicians are not sure of the shortest distance between two pints. You may still have to learn how much you can drink safely without suffering. If you throw up, suffer the whirling pit when you close your eyes, or cannot remember all of the previous evening, you really drank too much. In fact, you were probably pewted as a niss.

☺   The wages of gin is breath.   ☺

If you're on the beer, try to avoid quaffing it – that's similar to drinking it but you spill more. Be warned! Over-indulgence in alcohol is a particular danger in the first-year and causes many students to do badly. You might choose to stay away from binge drinking and all games that involve knocking back booze as a penalty – if you're present and a session starts up around you, try to keep it a personal spectator sport.

Clubs and societies
You will suddenly be faced with the opportunity to join lots of clubs. Go on! Join a few! Maybe a sports one for your health's sake (you don't have to be a rugger-bugger, soccer-rocker, or have a cricket-ticket); a social one for fun; and an intellectual or political one for interest and personal development. In the first week there will probably be something like a "Student Fair", with lots of stalls staffed by second or third-year students trying to get you to join their clubs. It's best to walk round and see them all before signing up. Try this as early in the week as possible because that's when people are making new friends and forming their initial social groups.

Any initial worries should quickly pass
It is normal to feel uncertain, insecure or just plain scared when you arrive at university. You do not know what it's about or what will be expected of you. Fear of the unknown can be powerful. You will probably also feel excited and exhilarated by the new opportunities. It can take a few weeks to settle down but most students manage to adapt. If this is your first time living away from home, expect to feel homesick, especially in the first few weeks. If you make some new friends quickly in Fresher Week it will help to reduce the problem. If you should feel a bit low in the first few days, call a close friend or two – it will improve your morale. You almost certainly have a mobile already, and you might be able to persuade your parents to pick up the bill or at least put some money in for the term "so I can call you more often".

FREEDOM MEANS CHOICES!

Choosing study rather than full-time fun
Freedom is a heady drug if you have come straight from school, particularly if it was a boarding school where the environment is carefully controlled. At university, all restrictions are removed and the choice of how you spend your time is entirely yours. You will rarely have compulsory lectures (although this depends on your university), and you can stay in bed all day if you wish. Be particularly careful not to spend the bulk of the first term drinking in the union bar, playing pool, and neglecting your studies. I know I'm repeating this but it's tempting and I've seen it happen so often.

How can you tackle this new seductive freedom? By
- Making your own weekly timetable.
- Making and carrying your daily list of tasks.
- Keeping an assignments diary; and especially
- Working to increase your motivation and determination.

Buddy can you spare the time? Your weekly schedule
You can draw up a seven-day schedule, hour by hour, starting with the earliest time of day you begin studying or attending class, and covering the period until you go to bed. When you've finished, stick it on the wall or somewhere you can easily see it. On this timetable you might want to use different colours for lectures, tutorials, workshops etc. to make it easy to read at a glance, but whatever works for you is best.

> ☺ When I see the sign "This door is alarmed" I realise that I feel a bit ☺ uneasy myself.

Contact time
In the humanities and the social sciences you might have as low as five formal contact hours a week, but more likely it will be eight to twelve hours. This is of course much less than you were used to at school or at work. Don't be fooled! This teaching period is only a fraction of the time you are expected to study – remember, you are supposed to learn on your own. Depending on the individual, for each one hour of formal teaching you might need to do around two to four hours of personal study for decent results. In law, medicine, engineering and the sciences you are

more likely to have a longer formal schedule to follow, maybe 16–25 hours a week or more.

Taking time off
How many evenings you work depends in part on your personal sleep cycle: some people wake late but are prepared to study until two a.m. Others wake naturally around five a.m. and study until breakfast about eight, which is equivalent to an evening's work on its own. For many people, the mornings are a particularly productive time.

A typical student who wants to do well can allow maybe two or three evenings a week off from study and take a day off at the weekend (maybe both days but only if you are really bright); those who just want a bare pass might take most evenings off as well as much of the weekend and gamble they get through. My suggestion is to err on the side of more study in the early days – it is easier to decide later to take more leisure than to force yourself to study harder. In your non-study time, it's a good idea to play some sport or at least engage in some very different and non-intellectual activity in order to relax. Go on, you can think of something that fits that description.

Assessing your timetable
When you've finished your draft timetable, add up the hours – if they are less than 40 a week, which a survey in 2006 showed is likely, you are not going to die from overwork. In 2004, full-time employees in Britain typically worked 44 hours a week, while one in six put in more than 60 hours, a figure typical for many professionals. Try to balance your subjects so that you do not fall behind anywhere; later you can adjust your work schedule if you find you are dropping behind in a particular subject. Remember to allocate time for "assignment research" as you will have new essays etc. coming up. And I know that you will remember to allow yourself some relaxation time.

Making a daily list of tasks
It helps if you carry a list of what you intend to do each day. The list should include the time and place of your lectures, tutorials, seminars, workshops or lab sessions, as well as what you intend to do in your personal study time. You might set aside a special half an hour for practising drawing diagrams, revising vocabulary lists or whatever your particular subject needs; some time for going over

the day's notes; and say half an hour for revision of things done earlier in the term. Carry your daily list with you and don't forget to check it regularly. Cross off each item when you've done it and enjoy the feeling of achievement and success. If the first item on your list is "make list" you can cross that one off almost immediately and feel good.

☺   Warning: dates in the calendar arrive faster than you might expect!   ☺

Keeping an assignments diary
It's a good idea to note in your diary when assignments are due, and also flag them in advance early enough to prepare. Depending on your subject, your abilities and the rest of your timetable, you might need maybe three or four days for short essays and perhaps a week or two for longer items. Adjust your lead-time as necessary.

Working to increase your motivation
See the section "Whether you're young or old, strengthen that motivation!", page 39, for advice on working to boost your determination. This is really an important thing to do and the sky's the limit, sport!

DECIDING THE ESSENTIALS: HOUSING, TRANSPORT, FOOD AND FINANCE

The housing and transport problems need tackling early, while the food problem largely depends on what you decide to do about the first two issues.

Choosing where to live

☺   Don't expect too much...   ☺

Home is the cheapest
Living at home is a good option if you get along with your family and are going to your local university. In England it used to be pretty standard to go to a university in a different city, but it is now becoming common to go to one nearby as it's cheaper. If you go locally but are not living at home, your parents may invite you for meals, including that important Sunday lunch, and help you in other ways. They probably have a washing

machine and ironing board and maybe your mum will be sympathetic enough to use these on your behalf! On the other hand, going away can be more fun and you will grow up faster.

University accommodation
University accommodation is often located relatively close to the university itself, and transport may be easier. Such accommodation is often the best choice in the first-year – halls of residence are great and you have a ready-made social group. To get a place you should apply as early as you can. On weekdays they usually supply breakfast and an evening meal, plus all three meals at the weekend. The food will not be fantastic but it should be adequate. Petty thieving can sometimes be a problem so it's wise to lock your door if you leave your room, even briefly. Sadly, you might find that you have to move out after a year to make room for the new first-year students, so enjoy it while you can.

Unlike the residential halls, a university flat means you will have to cook for yourself, maybe sharing a kitchen with a few other students, but at least you are with your own species.

> ☺ Q. How many Australian students does it take to change a light bulb?
> A. Five – one to hold the bulb and four to drink beer until the room spins.

Private accommodation
Private accommodation is a common choice for your second or third-year – you might get a bed-sitter or share a house. Bed-sitters are not the best option for first-year students and potential problems include:
- Being located in a non-student area. (I tried it, it was awful!)
- Being located in an area where street violence occurs. (Worse! Only a peanut might wish to be assaulted.)
- Poor food (if supplied) or otherwise having to shop and cook for yourself.
- Loneliness and a feeling of being isolated from all your friends and the Uni.
- Being with an unpleasant family or bad landlord. (Miserable!)

If you find things are not working out in your bed-sitter, find alternate accommodation before you tell them you're leaving. You can expect not to be popular as they are about to lose a regular source of income – your rent.

Sharing a house or flat is often a good bet in your second or third-year, when you are more experienced and you can be with friends you choose. It may be worth paying a little extra in rent to get into a nice place in a good location where you will be happy and can get to the Uni and parties easily and without huge transport costs. Remember, the larger the group, the cheaper per head, but the greater the noise and distraction. In a large house, a silent night may prove to be more of a Christmas carol than a reality (see also "Housing", page 10).

☺   Last night as I lay in bed looking at the stars I thought, "Where the   ☺
       hell is the ceiling?"

Sharing a house or flat can have problems such as
- Finding suitable flat-mates can be hard.
- Some people turn out to be impossible to live with and disputes will arise.
- Rostered duties (cooking; cleaning) may be, or more likely will be, ignored – leading to hell's smells and buckets of crud.
- Food disappears and everyone looks innocent: suddenly it's Mother Hubbard time.
- Meanwhile ancient food icki-fies in the fridge and no one cleans it out.
- The phone bill always seems to be higher than the calls people admit to making; a mobile each and no landline can solve that one.
- The only tidy person in a house of slobs tends to do all the cleaning and tidying.
- An obsessive cleaner annoys us slobs.
- You may have bug problems that attack your food, your clothes, or even you.
- Some houses and flats can be in poor condition (especially damp; inadequate bathroom or kitchen; poor electrical wiring; or old and dangerous gas fires).
- Getting the share of the rent and electricity from everyone is not easy.
- The kitty for communal goods (washing up liquid etc.) empties rapidly.
- The cost of setting up is high and will include a deposit and rent in advance.

- The impromptu midnight party with strangers sounds better than it really is.
- It is too easy to get distracted and not study when there are several other students around.
- In some areas, burglars and thieves seem to target student houses.

Minimum things you will need for the place

You might find that you need bedding, an alarm clock, an iron, cutlery, plates, mugs, a kettle, one or two sauce-pans and frying pans (ever wondered how they get that non-stick finish to cling on?), cleaning materials, and maybe a bucket and a broom. A sleeping bag or two might be useful if people sleep over, as with any luck they will! A Swiss army knife can also prove useful: you can open beer, open cans, pick your teeth – even cut things if necessary. The actual knife fittings vary a lot so choose one to suit your needs – the angling one with a hook disgorger is of less value to a clarinet player.

If no departing students are trying to offload their stash, you can try a charity shop, car boot sales, or weekend markets for second-hand serviceable stuff. Oh! And when you finally leave as a group, try to get everybody to help clean the place thoroughly and really make the flat or house glisten. This will substantially improve your chances of getting your deposit back.

Beam me up, Scotty: dealing with the problem of transport

If you don't get into university accommodation, it is essential to consider the issue of transport when choosing where to live. Try to get on or near a public transport route that goes directly to the university – having to make a change wastes heaps of time. Ask about public transport passes, which can save you a lot of money. Freshers sometimes get special deals, and if you are offered one by a reliable company with good schedules, they are often worthwhile.

If you can honestly pose the question "Dude, where's my car?", consider sharing rides and getting a contribution towards petrol and other costs – you can advertise on notice-boards around the university. To deter thieves, never leave anything visible in your car and fit an anti-theft device. A visible steering wheel lock is actually not hard to deal with but it encourages the thief to move on and try somebody else's vehicle. Never make it easy for them! Motorbikes are cheaper to buy and run than cars but are more dangerous.

Bicycles are even cheaper, and many students rely heavily on their bike, but they too can be dangerous. Buy a crash helmet (you can leave it in your locker usually and it's better than vegetating in hospital) as well as the best lock and chain you can afford (definitely cheaper than replacing your whole bike). Don't forget to lock your bicycle to something solid and take all removable parts with you when you leave. In some areas it is wise to lock both wheels to the frame.

☺ And before we leave transport, are we meant to take seriously that ☺ intriguing road sign "Humps for 600 yards"?

Eating cheaply

Living in a hall of residence
You will probably have to buy lunch at the university unless you have somewhere to keep food that you can take in with you. Some students find it saves money if they force down as big a breakfast and evening meal as possible and eat little or nothing at lunchtime. It is not a good health practice but they do it anyway.

Cooking for yourself – be a fat boy or be slim?

Learn to make your own burger – it's cheaper and tastes heaps better!

Eating in restaurants is usually not cheap and too often neither is the refectory. In particular, sausages and meat pies are rarely good value: there is relatively little meat in them (if you ignore the stuff they put in like the animal's nose, lips and ears – yuck!) and this makes sausages and pies an unusually expensive way of buying protein. Commercial hamburgers are not particularly good value either. To keep costs down, buy good quality mince and an onion and prepare your own – it's your money and you can put it where your mouth is. Adding cheese, tomato, bacon or a fried egg

14

appeals to gluttons like me. Moreover, I add gently-fried garlic but I have to try to breathe only on enemies, not my friends.

Buy unwashed potatoes for preference as they are less expensive, then wash or peel them yourself. Generally, it saves your scarce cash if you buy the raw materials and prepare your own meals even if you have to learn to cook a bit. If you are new to cooking, buy a beginner's cookbook and make sure it explains the terms it uses, like "sauté" or "parboil". Unless you have some experience, you should avoid any book that says things like "Prepare the cabbage in the usual way…" or "Cook until tender" without indicating how long you are likely to be hanging around.

Try books like Cas Clarke, *More Grub on Less Grant*, or her *Essential Student Cookbook;* or else Joy May, *Nosh 4 Students*. Both authors suggest cheap and easy-to-cook meals. If there are only one or two of you there is an exception to the rule that it is cheaper to buy the raw materials and do it yourself. Those pre-packed supermarket salads can work well; buying a few different whole lettuces means you end up throwing away a lot of rotting leaves because of the quantity problem.

A curry is easy to make once you've bought the spices – and some like it hot. Note that spices lose flavour with time, so it's a good idea to buy those you will use regularly and avoid recipes that require a peculiar spice that you might rarely use again. While on the subject, check out the local curry restaurants to see if any offer an "all-you-can-eat" buffet for a fixed price; if you have a healthy appetite these can be incredibly good value.

Vegetarian dishes using beans are nutritious and are cheap to make at home – but eat too many and you could be gone with the wind.

☺   Give peas a chance.   ☺

Left-overs make good cheap eating, and if you deliberately roast or boil more potatoes than you want, you can eat them cold or fry them up for a later meal. Similarly, a roast can supply you with several meals including sandwiches. If you roast a chicken (easy to do!), keep all the bones and bits of gristle from meal times, boil the bits up with the carcass and then simmer for an hour or two with some chopped-up root vegetables and a few herbs to make a great soup. If it tastes thin, boil it so it reduces in volume until it tastes nice. Adding a cup of rice or lentils (needing maybe an hour plus) bulks it out and makes it a lot more filling.

Do not miss out on breakfast, as this can reduce your energy to study and to enjoy yourself. "Bread and…." meals are not all that good for you, particularly if eaten all the time. If you must, peanut butter is not a bad spread especially if you smear jam or honey on top of it. Some scrape

Marmite on it, but some people will do anything. A big muesli breakfast is good and very filling, and unless you happen to be Audrey Hepburn beats Tiffany's hollow. Muesli is improved if you add some nuts and chopped up dried or fresh fruit of your own (a ripe banana – yesss!) and this will not make you a cereal killer. Use strong scissors to cut up nuts and dried fruit to a manageable size. This is a good way of making a boring muesli more interesting and, let's be honest, if you don't like the muesli you probably won't eat it. You should buy the best muesli you can; it may look more expensive but on a per meal basis, the difference is minuscule. When the chips are down, it's best to avoid a lot of fried food.

Money, money, money

Since the 1980s, the government has increased student numbers but tried to contain educational expenditure, in part by charging fees and forcing students to take out loans rather than giving them adequate grants. You will almost certainly need more money than you will get.

Other than drawing on existing savings, your possible sources of finance are grants, parental contributions, loans, a part-time job or, for a fortunate few, sponsorship by a company. Robbing banks and blackmailing friends are not recommended solutions. Incidentally, if you are a member of a trade union, it is worth checking the rules to see if they offer any educational assistance.

When borrowing, try your relatives first – they are likely to waive interest, or at the worst charge a very low rate. The government makes student loans available – ask for details in your university (and see "Borrowing" below, page 18).

☺   Students, like bakers, need a lot of dough.   ☺

Choosing a bank account
Many university entrants will have to open their first bank account. You may find a bank stall at the Fresher Fair but you should not automatically sign up. It is common for a bank to offer money to the students' union to be allowed to set up a stall and you might easily get a 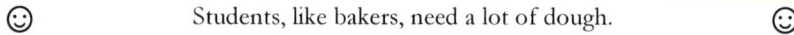better deal elsewhere. Shop around: as you will probably go into debt, you need to know about those all-important overdraft limits and interest rates. These will matter more to you than their bribes – that enticing free Ipod or MP3 player may look attractive but you might save so much in lower interest rates at a different bank that you could buy your own kit and still come out ahead.

On the other hand, some banks offer free travel vouchers which can be valuable if you live some distance away from Uni.

Finance and the more mature student
Mature students often have financial commitments over and above day-to-day living expenses; the following are some way of helping to deal with these.
- If you have dependent children, you can claim benefits from the state while you are at university.
- If you are paying off a mortgage, think about changing to an interest-payment-only version for your three years at university, as this will reduce your monthly outlay.
- Have you a marketable skill that will allow you to earn part-time?
- Can you get a part-time job somewhere you worked before?
- Do you have any relatives or other contacts who can offer you work?

EVERYONE SHOULD MAKE THE MOST OF FRESHER WEEK

Surviving your first day
Registering as a student and getting your National Union of Students card are normally all that really matter on your first day. The rest largely consists of you hanging about waiting for things to happen and being talked at by a variety of people. Usually not a lot of what you are told is truly important, but you could take a notepad and pen to write down anything that you might want to remember.

The best reason for going on the first day is to make new friends while standing in queues or just sitting around. You do not want to be alone on your first evening – you really have to meet up with friends then. There might be a disco organised, or a film show; but if you do not hear about anything special, drop by the student union for advice on what's on. And try hard not to make your first Saturday the loneliest night in the week either – a rhapsody in blue is not for you. If you are in university accommodation, sitting with your door open attracts casual callers and you should meet people easily. If there is free tea, coffee or cocoa offered at a set time – go! I guarantee there will be others anxious to talk to you.

Taking out insurance
Your travel card is not the only thing that might get swiped, and too many students have some of their possessions stolen. It's a good idea to check your parents' home contents policy to see if you are covered while away – it might be included already but if the company wants a little higher premium there is a good chance your parents will pay the extra themselves. If they do, you have probably saved more than the cost of this book already and are ahead of the game. Well done you!

Borrowing
The majority of students borrow money. If you have to do so, check first with the Student Loan Company (SLC – see Appendix A for the Internet address) as their loans are low interest – and interest free until you leave your course. You do not have to start to repay the loan until the April after graduation; repayments are done via the income tax system. SLC loans are renowned for arriving late, so you are advised to apply early – March is the earliest allowed. You can approach a bank, but overdrafts are more expensive than the SLC loans. You can also ask your university for financial help.

Apart from such necessity loans, if you are just starting in life, it can be a good idea to borrow a small amount from a bank, say £100, *but do not spend it*. Instead, use it all to repay the loan on time. If you do this once or twice, it starts to build you a good credit rating so that when you really do need money you can get it more easily. It is even possible to make money like this, by borrowing at a low interest from the government body then investing it in a high interest savings account until you need it. Remember! You did not read that here.

Making a budget
You should make a weekly budget and try hard to stick within it. For the first month you should keep a track of how you really spend your money as opposed to how you plan to. Adjust your budget and expenditure as needed.

Try to avoid those pesky credit cards
It's best not to accept a credit card. It is too dangerous a temptation to spend and you are likely to run up debts that you cannot repay. If you already have such a card, why not grab a pair of scissors now and cut it up? In contrast, a cashpoint card is handy and means you can get out small amounts of money when you need to.

Getting a part-time job
You will probably need to take a vacation job to survive. You might have to consider taking a part-time job during the term too, probably in the evenings or at the weekend. Typically, you can expect to earn about the legal minimum wage and work maybe ten hours a week – if you can find a job. Bar work is popular, pulling beer and the occasional customer. You can ask at your student union office if they know of any local firms who hire, or you can approach the university employment officer if there is one. Also, talk to other students, read the adverts in the local newspaper and keep an eye open for notices in shops, cafes and pub windows.

You might find something online at JustJobs4Students – it's worth a try. You can also look at the government's site Jobcentre Plus but do not expect too much (see Appendix A for both). If you take work as a tutor or with some charity it might help you find a better job when you graduate because it improves your CV.

Be aware that if you work in term you lower your chances of getting a good degree. A study showed that for those working 15 hours a week, the odds of getting a first or upper second were a mere 62 per cent of similar but non-working students.

☺ The first law of philosophy: for each philosopher there is an equal and opposite philosopher. ☺

Living cheaply
Don't be a fashion victim; looking glamorous might have its attractions but can prove costly. It's a mistake to buy new fashionable clothing unless you are determined to look good at all costs. Fashion gear tends not to last too long, either because it is badly made of cheap material or because fashions change and eventually you may start to feel that you would not be seen dead in it again. You do not have to look like a fashion plate while studying – dressing simply in sturdy clothing is cheaper. You might decide that you only need one decent outfit, perhaps to wear at an annual dance or maybe at somebody's wedding. If so, and you think that you are rarely

Figure 1. Tips for living cheaply

- If you have a hobby, put it aside for your university years – it will cost you money.
- Never go shopping for fun – only buy what you really need rather than simply want - and stay away from special sales.
- Never wear a T-shirt that says "If found return to nearest shopping mall".
- Never buy something merely because it is cheap or on special offer, unless you were planning to buy it anyway.
- Buying ready-made food is dearer than making your own from scratch.
- Avoid ordering delivered pizza and other foods; there is always a delivery charge even if it is invisibly built into the price.
- A small joint is easy to roast and you can get several meals off one.
- Buy in supermarkets – but ignore the impulse buys near the till. Check out what they have on special but see that it is not almost on or even past its use-by date (some people will try it on!).
- Buying bottled water can be expensive around the university and town; if you carry a small screw-top bottle you can refill it at a tap for free.
- Rather than buy a newspaper every day, you can read one or two in the library.
- And if you are a smoker – stop now and save a small fortune!
- Dishwashers are expensive to use; best do it by hand.
- If you have a fridge, always decide what you want to take out before you open the door.
- Turn off the lights when leaving an otherwise empty room.

going to wear the outfit, it is usually cheaper to hire something you like, even though on the surface it may seem an extravagance.

It's not a bad idea to spend as little as possible on clothes for the next three years. Buy in charity shops unless you have a "thing" about second-hand clothes. Clothing often makes up a surprisingly high percentage of people's spending and offers great scope for economising.

Keeping warm offers possibilities for saving too. In winter, it is cheaper to wear more clothes (several layers work best – double knit, pure wool sweaters, warm or what?) or do a bit of exercise than turn up the central heating or switch on an electric fire. The university library is a warm place to be and you can study comfortably there. If you're really freezing, bed is a good place to keep warm even if you're home alone.

Try to find free or cheap entertainment where possible – good places to look include the student newspaper and the local rag. Listening to the radio and watching TV is free once you have a set. If you're in a hall of residence it probably has a TV room. If sharing a house, somebody's parents might be persuaded to give you their old set and buy themselves a new one (remember that you need a licence!). In addition, you can try looking at the goods offered on the Freecycle site in your local area (see Appendix A) and you can advertise there for what you want. As the stuff is all free, be aware that good items get snapped up very quickly. See Figure 1 for more tips on saving money.

☺   The second law of philosophy: they're both wrong.   ☺

Using the rest of Fresher Week
Use any spare time to find out where things are: the student union and what is in it; the refectory; all the other eating and coffee places around campus; the commercial outlets like shops, the bookshop, a bank, a post office or whatever; and the library. If you are new in town look at a map and learn your way around. It is useful to know the local entertainment possibilities, including cafes and pubs. You can also check out the transport system and bus routes – try to get a bus map, and find out about the last bus or the late night service.

You will need some kind of bag to carry your books and notes around, but don't rush out and buy that expensive briefcase immediately. A free supermarket bag (using two together is stronger) will do for a few days until you decide what you want. Similarly, if you are given reading lists this early, do not race out and buy all the books suggested. You will probably not need to own them all (see the section on "Getting to grips with the set textbook" in Chapter 3, page 50). It is useful to look at the latest university handbook and read the general information section – it will answer some of your questions and help to ease your passage into this new and exciting life. The book isn't usually worth buying and the university library will have a copy available.

Socialising
Yes, it's the fun part! Remember that university is primarily for you to learn and you want that degree. However, you are positively encouraged to go overboard in this first week and enjoy yourself; try to make lots of friends and start to build a social group for when the studying and learning really begin. Remember to go to all (or most) of the organised entertainment like discos or student hops that are held in Fresher Week and don't mope around on your own.

DON'T WASTE YOUR FIRST-YEAR!

In some universities, the work done in the first-year does not count directly towards the degree, which encourages some students to laze around, watch a lot of day-time TV, drink too much, and generally not work hard. It's a trap! Don't let this happen to you! First-year work lays the foundation for a good degree. It's like building a wall: can you imagine how easy it would be to build the top half, if the bottom half were wonky and with bits missing? It's an ongoing process and really is education by degrees. However, if you decide not to aim for a good degree and just want any old one (mistake! mistake!), it will still be easier if you work in year one and then relax a bit in later years as you will have a solid foundation and good habits in place.

CASE STUDIES

Let us introduce three students of different backgrounds and abilities whom we will follow in subsequent chapters. Each has different strengths and weaknesses in their experience, personality, and adjustment to university life.

Aziz Ahmad needs less out of Fresher Week
Aziz is 32 years old and lives with his wife and child. He recently spent a year living and working abroad, so he has fewer problems of adjusting to

new circumstances. He goes to all the introductory sessions and joins three clubs (drama, squash and film). He is a bit worried about whether he can afford university but is confident that he will succeed. He didn't participate in many Fresher Week activities, because he is married, has many outside friends, and isn't seeking a social life in the university.

At this stage Betty Lin's social life does not look all that promising
Betty is from Singapore and moved here with her parents when she was 6 years old. She is now 19 and lives with her parents. She is rather unassertive, slow to make friends, and often tends to feel a bit of an odd girl out. She is intelligent and hard working but still worries about succeeding. She spent a year working in a bank before she came to university but made few friends among her colleagues. On her first day at Uni she goes straight home after registration ends and sits reading the stuff she has been given. During the week she finds out where everything is, but she doesn't join any clubs so that socially she is already not getting as much as she could out of university.

Naughty by nature: Charlie Jones's social life is already looking good
Charlie is 18 years old, comes straight from school and manages to get into a hall of residence. He joins six clubs on the first day (including a specialised boozing group); this is his first taste of freedom and he is determined to enjoy it – and is already on the track to wasting time. On the first night he goes clubbing outside the university, where he drinks too much and wipes himself out. On the plus side, he already knows a dozen people at Uni and has picked up an invitation to a party next weekend.

DISCUSSION POINTS

1. Are your reasons for going to university the same as those of your friends? Can you think of ways to associate your own reasons for going with ways of increasing your motivation? How else can you strengthen your will to work?

2. What sort of job do you hope to do and what skills (as opposed to knowledge) would help you to succeed in it?

3. How many hours do your parents or a friend of yours work each week? How does this compare with your timetable?

SUMMARY

- A strong will to succeed is important; try to do things to increase your motivation.
- Those who do well go to all the sessions, study on their own, and use their time effectively.
- University means a new life style for you – and some adjustments.
- The sudden freedom is exhilarating but can be hard to cope with.
- Excessive drinking and socialising are dangers for some.
- Your initial worries and uncertainty will quickly pass.
- Sort out your housing and transport problems early.
- Adjust your behaviour in order to live cheaply.
- Join a few clubs at once and make friends as fast you can.

2. Now I'm here, what am I supposed to do?

> Myself when young did eagerly frequent
> Doctor and Saint, and heard great argument
> About it and about: but evermore
> Came out by the same Door as in I went
> (Edward Fitzgerald, *The Rubaiyat of Omar Khayyam*, xxvii)

THE LOW-DOWN ON HIGHER LEARNING

Your university really has only two main goals
One aim is to pass on existing knowledge to a new generation so that nothing is forgotten – this means teaching you. The other is to push back the frontiers of knowledge – this means research. A third function has emerged since the 1980s – raising money. Academics are now expected to bring in extra cash for the university from consultancy or research, as governments become stingier.

☺ Q. What's the difference between a historian and an engineer? ☺
A. About £45,000 a year.

Seeing how your department fits into the university

The organisation of the university
Most universities have a similar structure but may use slightly different names. At the very top is a governing body, often called a senate or council, which is legally responsible for the whole institution and decides the major policies. It meets perhaps once a month for maybe three hours. There is usually a Chancellor whose function is largely honorary but carries great prestige. The person who really runs the place is the Vice-

Chancellor. He is "Mister Big" and you will probably never meet yours. Below him, there are often several Deans, each in charge of a faculty. A faculty is a grouping of similar disciplines. Under that level there will be several departments, each with its own departmental head. In newer universities, instead of departments there may be schools, either under the faculty level or sometimes replacing it entirely.

☺   Governing body = to be in charge of a corpse.   ☺

The faculty side
The people who teach and do research are called faculty staff. At the top are professors, followed by associate professors or readers, then senior lecturers, lecturers, assistant lecturers and maybe teaching assistants. A department head might be a professor, senior lecturer or even a lecturer. "Doctors" are people who have earned a PhD as opposed to "Mr, Ms, Miss or Mrs" who have not done one. To gain a PhD requires much research, leading to the writing of a thesis that must be both original and deal with something that matters academically. It takes a minimum of three years, often more. A university might also require some course work be taken – this is normal in the United States, but less so in the UK.
Unless told otherwise, you can address Professors and Associate Professors as "Professor X" and anyone else with a doctorate as "Doctor X".

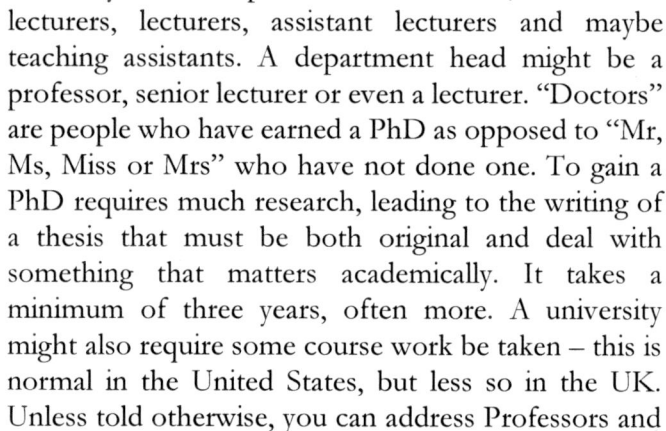

The administrative side
The administration runs the university for the staff and students. At the top is the registrar who controls all the various departments that keep the place clean, run the library and refectory, pay the staff salaries, and so forth.

☺   You can always tell a bureaucrat but you can't tell him much.   ☺

There is often a hidden battle going on between some of the academics and some of the administrators, but we don't talk about it openly. In fact, you don't even know about it.

WHY AM I HERE? MANY PHILOSOPHERS HAVE ASKED THIS

Well you're here to get a degree – and in the process, enjoy yourself. This really means the following.

Gaining knowledge and developing skills
First, you will gain knowledge and develop skills through a relatively small number of formal teaching sessions. You spend (whoops! *should* spend) a lot more time going off to learn informally on your own or with others.

Assessment
Second, you are assessed to check that you have reached an acceptable level. You write essays, present oral assignments, sit exams and the like. When you are thought to be good enough you get your degree. For most, it is a Bachelor of Arts (BA) or Bachelor of Science (BSc) and normally takes three years, although four year degrees are coming in.

Most students in England do an honours degree, and they get one of the following levels:

- First class (a first).
- Upper Second class (a two-one).
- Lower Second class (a two-two).
- Pass (a third).
- Fail.

Above this first degree level, there is the Master of Arts (MA), Master of Philosophy (MPhil) and Master of Science (MSc) all of which take a year or two; the Masters can be done by pure research (MRes) which involves writing a major dissertation. Above this level is the Doctor of Philosophy (PhD) which few bother to do unless going to work in universities. The degree of Doctor of Science (DS) may be awarded to a few academics, based upon their published articles and books; this degree is falling into disuse in the UK.

Formal teaching sessions
For the formal learning time you are supposed to:
- Attend various teaching sessions (lectures, tutorials etc.), listen and take notes.
- Submit some written assignments (essays, quizzes, tests etc.).

- Present some oral assignments (tutorial or seminar papers, project reports, or role-playing presentations).
- Perhaps do some workshops or lab work.

Informal learning
In your informal learning time, you should:
- Read books and journal articles in the library and take notes.
- Read and learn the notes you have taken in lectures and elsewhere.
- Discuss, debate, and argue passionately with anybody you can find – it's important to do this!

Reading the information supplied
You will settle down more quickly if you look at what you are given. Much of what may puzzle you at first is often described in handouts – the trouble is that you may get so many of these that you might not actually read them, or else forget what is in them. When you have a question, it is a good idea to check your bumf first to see if someone has already given you the answer.

The must-do part: lectures, tutorials, seminars, workshops and lab sessions

Lectures
Lectures are designed to pass information to you in an efficient way. In a large university there can be a lot of people in the lecture room, perhaps several hundred in your first-year. In the beginning, the lectures may consist largely of mainstream knowledge, but in the second and third-year they often contain much original information. Lectures do not often blindly follow the textbook, and you should not be surprised if you find the set text being criticised. You may be allowed to ask questions in lectures, and if you are not clear whether this is the case you should ask. You need to take notes.

☺   Subdued = a less than cool guy.   ☻

Tutorials
One-staff-to-one-student tutorials have become a definite luxury and not many universities can afford them. These days, tutorials usually consist of a staff member and if you are lucky maybe half a dozen students – but more recently the students might number anything up to 30 or so. A

student reads out a previously prepared short essay paper while you listen. You should note down any questions and comments which you would like to ask during the discussion that will follow. The tutor leads the discussion and might sum up at the end. The purpose of tutorials is to encourage you to think for yourself, discuss what you have heard, criticise views, and put ideas into context. Do try to participate – it's a valuable learning process in itself where you can gain valuable job skills.

Figure 2. A checklist of questions for the end of each week
(Reading this checklist regularly can help to increase your motivation)

- Did I attend all the recommended lectures, tutorial sessions and workshops etc.?
- Did I spend at least 10 minutes a day learning diagrams, vocabulary lists, formulae, or other items relevant to my course?
- Have I studied the relevant parts of the textbook in each subject that I am studying?
- Did I find the time to read over and learn some of my old notes as revision?
- Am I up-to-date with items that I have to submit?
- Did I get into the library to read the set texts?
- Did I get into the library to dig out information for myself?

Seminars
Seminars are more often given to larger groups than tutorials, but work in a similar way; sometimes they are a bit more formal. They tend to occur in later years or at the post-graduate level where the numbers attending might be relatively small.

Workshops and lab sessions
There are many things that can be done in workshops, depending on the subject being studied. You will receive help from the member of staff present who will tell you what to do and then let you loose. Workshops vary a lot in how they operate, but the constant factor is that you do something rather than sit and listen. You may have to do mathematical exercises, answer multiple-choice questions, participate in small group discussions of previously assigned material, engage in role-playing, or

work with apparatus – stuff like that. Some workshops can involve a lot of amusement and seem like fun rather than work.

Lab sessions are common in science, engineering and psychology and similarly require effort from you, often working with apparatus or, in some disciplines, observing what is going on. Again, the staff member will explain what you must do.

Research indicates that people who interact with information and actively do something remember up to four times as much as if they are simply told the information. The message is clear: make it easy on yourself and always go to workshops and tutorials and then participate strongly.

Learning your tutorial, lab and lecture notes
Notes are of no value until you read and learn them. Having taken the darn things it's no good filing them away to be forgotten. You should read your notes regularly and revise, learning as you go. If you forget to do this for some time, don't despair! This is "best advice" and you can start to read your old notes any time you want.

☺   To prepare a seminar: take one nar and divide it in half.   ☺

THERE'LL BE SOME CHANGES MADE

Building a network of friends and support groups
A network of friends is essential if you are to avoid loneliness, prevent feelings of depression or home-sickness, and generally enjoy yourself as you adapt to university life. You might already know some people who came to the university with you who immediately provide a social group. However, you will keep meeting people and develop new friends, so that as time passes you will probably find that you drift away from the original ones and strike out in new directions. It's normal: go for it!

Finding a study-buddy or study-group can make learning easier
A study-buddy (a naff phrase but an invaluable help) is virtually essential for easy and enjoyable learning. Working alone in individual competition has been traditionally regarded as normal but you can do much better if you find a friend

with whom to work closely. If you do this, you will settle down more quickly, learn more easily, and increase your level of motivation. It may be harder to locate a good one than finding Nemo, but you should try to do this early on (see the section on "Working with a good study-buddy or group is the fast track to learning", page 48).

Study-groups can be even more useful. They comprise a set of like-minded people who get along together and are doing the same course. They meet together and help each other learn. I recommend that you join a group – or start one if necessary.

OK – some study groups are more fashionable than others.

AND YOU THINK YOU'VE GOT PROBLEMS?

Academic problems
If you find you are not keeping up with the work, failing to read the assigned material, not getting essays in on time and the like, then examine your conscience. Have you been lazy? (Be honest!) If so, the solution is simple: work harder. If not, you probably need to reduce your leisure activities, increase your total work hours, and perhaps reallocate time on your weekly list towards a subject in which you are falling behind. You should definitely try to work more efficiently too. Try the techniques described in Chapters 3 and 4 below. Reminder! If you have not got one yet, find that study buddy, or join/start a study-group.

Financial and personal problems: don't you just hate them?
You should always seek help with financial and personal problems. Just telling someone about it can be of assistance and bring relief: both the religious confessional and psychiatrist's couch have provided peace of mind to many. Your problems may fall into areas like financial, emotional, social, family, or be connected with health or drugs. Frequently there will be a mixture of several problems because they tend to reinforce each other.

Seeking advice – you can get help from:
- Your personal tutor.
- Your university student counselling service or welfare officer (the name varies).
- The university health service nurse or doctor.
- The student union.
- Your partner (if you have one).
- Personal friends and support groups.
- Your local religious leader (if you are a member of that particular belief).
- Your parents (if your relationship permits).
- Your bank manager (financial).

☺ While at university, try to drink from the fountain of knowledge – merely gargling will not serve you as well. ☺

Dealing with the advice
It is wise not simply to accept the first counsel offered but to think it over carefully. It also pays to get suggestions from more than one source and compare what you have been told. In the end, you must make your own decision as to what to do.

Coping with sexual harassment
It is sometimes hard to recognise sexual harassment even though physical touching, stroking and patting are easy to identify, as is verbal abuse. Some jokes and the kind of language used may qualify as harassment. This is a rapidly changing and difficult area – values are in the process of altering, and not everyone accepts the same set, particularly if from a different age group or culture. My personal views are that if a member of your peer group tells you that you are pretty, handsome, sexy etc., this is not harassment, it is only "an offer to treat" (as lawyers say with unconscious irony) and ultimately helps to keep the human race going. Harassment seems to involve repetition and a refusal to stop after you have said no or otherwise made it clear that you do not welcome the advances. If the approach is from an authority figure above you (a professor or the like) then that is a different matter and is quite likely to constitute harassment.

If you are not sure if you are being harassed, go and talk to someone about it. You can ask in your departmental office if your university has a sexual harassment officer, enquire at the student union office, check with the women's group (if you are female) or talk to the people at the university medical centre. Do not forget that you can be sexually harassed by someone of the same sex too.

Coping with stress
There are many ways of coping with anxiety and worries. A religious belief can offer consolation, and your local minister, mullah, priest, or rabbi may offer valuable suggestions. Physical exercise is also a good way of releasing tension, either in organised sport or in an exercise regime on your own. Some find yoga to be particularly helpful. Different schools of meditation also offer ways of reducing levels of stress and you can try the various relaxation techniques described in Chapter 6, page 91.

If you feel the need to engage in self-harm, with a blade for example, or have trouble eating and keeping food down, you really must tell someone. You might find it impossible to inform your parents but your doctor is a good choice and your best friend could be a place to start. You *can* be reassured and helped to feel better about yourself and your life but it requires help from others. Don't try to go it alone.

☺ Bacchanalian = to put your money on an outsider in the space-race. ☺

ADJUSTING – THE CHANGE OF LIFE

For those coming straight from school
Your main problem in the first-year is likely to be coping with the new and exciting freedom. Ways of dealing with this were discussed in Chapter 1, page 8. Another short-term problem might well be the uncertainty that you may feel as you face the flood of new experiences. It is part of growing up to deal with uncertainty and incidents, then learn from your mistakes. Remember that you're not alone and everyone around you faces the same dilemmas, however well they may hide their fears. Although the initial novelty fades quickly, the whole of the first-year offers new experiences, so that the feelings of excitement and confusion may linger on for quite a while. You should try to see your time at Uni as an immense

and exhilarating opportunity, as well as a challenge – something you can enjoy while you grapple with and surmount the problems.

Dealing with bad study habits
At school, if you did not like a particular teacher you might have found that subject boring, you might have blocked the information being given to you, and not have worked hard at the subject. Conversely, if you liked the teacher, you probably did well at that subject. Henceforth you have no teachers, only a changing bunch of lecturers and tutors, so that personal liking or disliking is no longer relevant.

Some students develop another bad habit at school – they butter up to and flatter teachers in order to improve their personal standing and get better marks. If you found this a fast track to success, be aware those days are long gone. Only good written and oral assignments and exam results count now.

A different wile at school is to find out who will mark the paper and then write the answer you have reason to believe that the teacher expects. Goodbye to all that! Favouritism and conformity rarely count at university. In many courses, especially in large first-year classes, you may not even know who will mark your assignment and many of the staff will not know you.

Another common but unhelpful attitude involves trying to measure success by the degree of effort that went into an assignment, rather than the quality of the output. At university it is never any use complaining about a grade on the grounds you spent six weeks working hard on it. That is irrelevant. I could spend a year trying to do one painting as good as any by William Blake or Rembrandt and I would still fail dismally.

Adjustment for the mature student

☺ Think positive and don't despair: the combination of age and treachery mostly overcomes both youth and skill.   ☺

Boosting your self-confidence
You may feel insecure and uncertain, surrounded by all these bright eager youngsters. You might worry that you have been away from school too long and forgotten how to study. No problem! This book tells you how. You can get a degree and a good one; all you need is confidence and hard work – but you might have to keep reminding yourself of that. Age is not a barrier to learning and, although it is a bit harder to take in new things at fifty years of age than fifteen, it isn't that much harder. We know that people who go to university after they have been away from school score

better than those who go straight from school. And don't be afraid that you will be alone. Unless you are very unlucky, there should be plenty of people around your age – mature students attend university in increasingly large numbers.

Some older students fear that they will look foolish or lose face by expressing a wrong opinion. If you have been housebound for years, you may feel afraid to join in discussions or say what you think in case you are laughed at. Fight this feeling! You are more likely to find that the younger students take your word more seriously just because you are older and more experienced. In fact, they're often rather frightened of you, but will rarely admit it. As a mature student you have many strengths – read on and recognise them.

Maturity
Your greater age and experience of life mean that your attitudes are more developed and you are likely to make quicker and better decisions than young people. A sweat shirt I recently saw being worn by a female student said "next semester I'll be 35", so she did not seem to mind no longer being a teenager. In addition, you are not still in the process of growing up, or subject to hormonal changes that can produce sudden swings in emotions and moods, nor are you worried about the changes in your body and feelings. You might no longer be in the grip of an intense sexual force driven by the selfish gene and are probably not spending so much time dreaming about or pursuing those wonderful but elusive sexual partners.

☺   As Oscar Wilde once said: "I am not young enough to know   ☺
everything."

Motivation and the mature student
The determination to succeed is one of your main and sharpest weapons. You will be a lot more motivated than many youngsters: you really want to get that degree, you know what you are giving up in the form of income, and are aware of the costs in family terms. All this means you are prepared to work harder – and that is often worth more than mere youthful exuberance.

Experience and skills
You are probably able to notice interlinkages or causes and effects more easily than the less experienced fry swimming around you. On average, you will also have better communication skills and be generally more poised. The vicissitudes of life mean that you have had the rough corners knocked off, survived office politics or factory humour, and perhaps

coped with the rearing of children. When faced with new ideas and knowledge, many propositions that can startle an 18-year-old may seem commonplace to you. A major plus is that the experience and wider information you possess provide hooks on which you can easily hang new knowledge and so learn more easily.

Sources of information you may have open to you
You are likely to have more friends and relatives with different experiences that you can call on for help or with whom you can discuss issues – and don't forget your ex-colleagues from work.

A supportive partner
You are also more likely to have an understanding and helpful partner than the typical 18-year-old, and he or she probably allows you enough time to study as well as being able to strengthen your will to do so.

> ☺ Time and hairlines are inversely correlated: as one advances the other ☺ recedes.

Financial security
You will probably be more financially secure than those coming straight from school, which means that you may not need to take a part-time job and work to supplement your income. If you have to work, you will probably earn more per hour and so not have to work as long. You may also be able to afford to buy all the textbooks and other recommended material, whereas some of the young students will be forced to go without or rely on finding those elusive library copies.

Despite the advantages a mature student possesses, there are a few special areas that you might have to work at

Coping with a lower standard of living
Your income will be less than previously, perhaps substantially so, and we all find it painful to reduce our standard of living. You may have to give up eating out, and severely curtail spending on clothes and entertainment. If you have to stop smoking and limit your consumption of wine and spirits, so be it. It will hurt at first, so remind yourself the sacrifice will be worth it; think of the future and consider the better-paid jobs for which you will be eligible. Besides, smoking can be thought of as a disease that is usually cured by cancer, so you'll be better off in more ways than one.

Fighting feelings of inadequacy: we are not alone
Do not worry about any feelings of inadequacy or fear that you will be unable to get a degree. Keep telling yourself you will do it and shift your focus to the advantages you possess. Don't worry that you have forgotten how to study and have been away too long; OK, you will be rusty but your essential skill has not gone. It's a bit like riding a bicycle – after time away you can still do it, but it may take a bit of practice before you are able to do it as well again.

Avoiding monopolising discussions
If you happen to be one of the extrovert and assured mature students, be careful not to monopolise discussions as this tends to annoy people. A good group leader should prevent this, but young tutors often lack experience and if younger than you, they may find it hard to rein you in. Be aware that you can get a bad reputation for continually saying "when I worked in ...", and telling strings of anecdotes.

Finding a study-buddy matters more for you than for the youngsters
It will help you if you seek out someone about your own age with whom you can work and discuss your concerns. You are looking for a good, compatible study-buddy, not someone who whinges and complains – you need support, not membership of a mutual moaning society. Note: if you are already in a relationship, it's best to choose someone who will not provoke sexual temptations unless you like to live dangerously!

☺ Work hard and don't be a couch potato or you might get a chip on your shoulder. ☺

Learning by doing – the more the merrier
If you worry that your brain might find it slightly harder to take in new things, as part of the learning process you can compensate by actively doing stuff, rather than simply reading. To widen your approach, try:
- Condensing your notes regularly.
- Making your notes memorable by adding things like colour or (if you have the skill) small cartoons in the margin.
- Practising drawing diagrams, figures etc. from your textbook and lectures.
- Making up your own tables of relationships or whatever, from the textbook and lectures.
- Making flashcards of important vocabulary, diagrams, formulae etc. and going through them on the bus or elsewhere.

- Going to search in the library for your own information for a set period each day.
- Going through different textbooks and comparing explanations of the same point.
- Meeting daily with your buddy to explain what you have learned.
- When you get home, telling your partner what each lecture was about.

Sorting out your family relationships
This should be a main priority because a supportive partner will make learning a lot easier. Before you start at university, sit and discuss who will do what, e.g. pick up the children, cook the meals, wash up, shop, and clean the house. You might find it helps to make a roster so it is clear who is in charge of what at each time.

Despite your best efforts, you may have to cope with feelings of resentment from your family if you stay up half the night to finish an essay then sleep in the next day, particularly if you were rostered for some domestic task. It is imperative that you avoid letting things fester, and you might choose to set aside time, say every Sunday evening, to discuss how things are going, what irritates the others, and decide what adjustments can be made to put things right. Keeping the family happy, or at least out of active revolt mode, can only help you.

The possibility of shortening your course
With your experiences, you might find things you have achieved in the past can gain you credit towards a degree, so that you could finish more quickly. Activities like setting up and running a business, working in a foreign country, managing a department, or gaining professional qualifications might qualify. It is worth asking in your departmental office – you never know, you could get lucky.

WHETHER YOU'RE YOUNG OR OLD, STRENGTHEN THAT MOTIVATION! IT WILL HELP YOU TO LEARN

☺   Seen on a notice-board in Brisbane, Australia: "Daily floggings will continue until staff morale improves."   ☺

If you want to succeed, increasing your determination and developing self-discipline is the way to go. You can:

- Consciously fight the cunning suggestions your brain will throw up that it would be nice to watch TV, go for a drink, or in fact do anything rather than be forced into this boring old studying business.
- Remind yourself constantly of your reasons for coming to university – keep reading the list I hope you made in Chapter 1.
- Look at your weekly timetable and tell yourself how much you look forward to various periods of study (even if you don't). Saying aloud things like "I love learning about..." seems to help some people.
- Dwell on the benefits of the good job you intend to get when you finish your degree.
- Recognise the fact that university life is better than school or work and that you certainly do not wish to be thrown out.
- Consider what it is costing you to be at university in terms of money and time – and the need not to waste these.
- Think about the shame if you fail and drop-out, then have to go home and confess to friends and family.
- Work with a study-buddy or study-group on a regular basis.
- Stick up little notes where you can see them, like "Work!", "Only eight weeks to the exams!", or whatever you think might help you.
- Put up a photograph of some expensive object you would like to have some day – maybe an old sports car, a new Porsche, a penthouse in a big city, a round-the-world cruise in an ocean liner, ….. (fill in the blank for yourself).

Coping with computers

You need a computer for word processing (writing and printing) your assignments, for searching the Internet for information, and for receiving email. If you can afford it, get your own.

Assigning a password to get into it is a good idea, particularly for a laptop. If it gets stolen this really annoys the thief! But write down the password, possibly in some code and with no indication of what it is. A neat way of choosing a password is the old spy-game trick of a number like 17-6-4-5; this indicates page 17, line 6, words 4 and 5 in your favourite book. As long as you own a few books, it's darned hard to crack! Otherwise, choose a password and hide it carefully – a password with letters and numbers in, as well as mixed upper and lower case, is a lot safer than a simple word. If you have gone away to Uni, maybe you could leave the password at home with your parents. Never stick it on or near the computer.

And remember not to drink coffee or whatever near the keyboard, especially with a laptop – I know from experience that way disaster lies!

If you are a mature student and were educated before the widespread availability of personal computers you may well be afraid of them, but don't be! Older academics were not brought up with computers and they managed to learn. Computers are little more than fast, stupid toys that happen to be great fun as well as a tremendous help. You can learn to use one. After all, even the 1960s hippy generation has come to terms with this technology.

CASE STUDIES

Aziz's age and experience help his swift adaptation
Aziz is starting to fit in well – by the end of the first month his wife accepts his busy study periods but gets irritated now and then, especially because he joined the drama society and has already been cast in a play. He rehearses two evenings a week plus Saturday afternoons, and she feels put upon. They have discussed the problem and agree that he will be

responsible for preparing the Sunday dinner to compensate. He has sold his car and bought a bike which he uses to get to and from university and takes sandwiches in for lunch, both of which save money.

The academic work is going well, but...
Betty is not making many friends and is not as happy as she thought she would be; however she finds it difficult to discuss the problem with her parents. She is studying hard and really does enjoy the academic challenge. She spends most evenings in the library or working at home and reads over her notes while sitting on the bus. She takes sandwiches in, but treats herself to lunch on a Friday which, sadly, so far she has eaten alone. Her parents help her out with money if she needs anything badly enough.

Freedom's just another word, but there can be much to lose
Charlie is making heaps of friends but the freedom is going to his head and he is drinking too much, too often. He never works in the evenings and is often out with friends or in the union bar. He walks to and from the hall of residence. He does not eat lunch but instead has a couple of pints in the university bar most days. He has found his grant is disappearing rapidly and has been forced to get a job in a local pub working two evenings a week. At least he gets the odd beer bought him by the occasional generous customer.

DISCUSSION POINTS

1. Does your university allow you access to computers attached to a printer? Where are they located? Can you also get onto the Internet?

2. At school, what subjects did you do well at? Did you like the teacher? Did you do well in any subject where you did not like the teacher? Can you identify any other reasons why you did not do well in some subject?

3. Why is it undesirable to lie in bed all morning? Is it always a bad idea?

SUMMARY

- You need to spend more time studying on your own than in set sessions.
- Find a congenial person and become study-buddies.
- Join or start a study-group.
- Seek help if you have problems.
- If you are coming straight from school, the sudden freedom might prove to be a problem for you – if so, tackle it!
- Mature students have several advantages and do better on average than those coming straight from school.
- If you are a mature student, self-confidence and family problems may need special attention.
- Keep working to increase your motivation to study.

3. Learning well now means earning more later

Learning is an active process – you learn by going off and reading on your own, discovering information, deciding what you think and applying your knowledge to problems. You can learn a lot from arguing and discussing with other students. This contrasts with teaching, which for you is a passive thing that the staff do while you sit, listen and take notes. At university you are expected to spend more time learning on your own than being taught by others.

HOW DO I START?

When trying to grasp a new idea, theoretical model, or new information generally:
- First, you try to understand it.
- Second, you learn it – this should be done until you are able to explain it to someone else.
- Third, you try to criticise it, but only after you understand it.
- Fourth, you try to think of any questions the theory, idea etc. raises or has left unanswered.
- Fifth, you try to put it into perspective with other views etc. you might have and reach some conclusions.

TIPS TO MAKE YOUR LEARNING EASIER

There are a lot of things that you can do to make learning at university easier. A central element is boosting your will to succeed (see the section "Whether you're young or old, strengthen that motivation!", page 39). Before starting each new task, such as reading your textbook, tell yourself a few times "I will enjoy this and I want to do it well – and that degree will get me… (insert object of your desire)". This simple act may sound a trifle odd – but it can help you to focus more.

You need more reinforcement than concrete
As soon as is practical, read over any notes you have taken that day from lectures or other sources. This action will reinforce the information and help embed it in your brain more quickly. This can be a surprisingly effective process. You can also take the opportunity to make any scrawled parts more legible.

Just start, damn it!
Or as a French jazz musician might say: go man, toot sweet. If you are finding it hard to settle down to study, you might be able to ease yourself in and develop enthusiasm by doing some simple, study-related task first. You could for instance file yesterday's lecture notes, sharpen your pencils, or sort out your bag. There are many such tasks that can help to nudge your mind towards study mode. The important thing is to start and do something, and not sit around thinking that you cannot be bothered or that it's too hard. Try breaking any major task down into bite-sized chunks and then tackle it bit-by-bit. You might promise yourself a little treat, such as making a cup of coffee or eating a sweet, but you get it only after you have finished the first bit of the job. Then tackle the next stage, and so on, with another reward in store.

Read those notes – again! Again! And once more won't hurt!
Not only should you read over the notes you took earlier that day, it will also help you to go back and read some of the notes you made earlier in the term. It is a good idea to set aside some time each day for this purpose, perhaps 30 minutes or so. Most people gain more from reading over these earlier notes than spending an extra half hour taking new ones.

Try explaining to someone else what you have just read
This is an excellent practice and offers major benefits to you. As you do the reading, if you know you will have to explain it later to your study-buddy it concentrates the mind wonderfully. When you come to actually explain it,

you will discover your weak spots and be able to plug the holes. Many new teachers discover that they only really understand something properly when they have to teach it to others. Finally, the discussion with your buddy, including their explanation to you, helps to drive the information home.

You can also condense your notes
Gathering together all your notes on one topic, reading them over, and then condensing them down is a good way of ensuring you see the outline of the topic and can identify many of its elements. The process is valuable in itself, and as a bonus you get an excellent summary that you can use when revising and swotting for exams.

> ☺ There are three kinds of mathematicians: those who can count and ☺ those who can't.

Organising your time well
Warning: the term will fly past, so make the best use of your time. You need to break up your activities into manageable blocks. Few people can concentrate fully for over an hour without a break, and for some it can be as short as 25 minutes. Many students find that around 45 minutes works for them. Between study blocks, it is a good idea to relax by doing something completely different. In the break, try things like making coffee, tidying your bedroom, washing up, doing some stretches plus exercises, or taking a short brisk walk. Then you go back refreshed, able to take on the world. Experiment and decide what sized time blocks fit you best, then organise your learning schedule to match.

You might also consider which is the best part of the day to study. Some people are morning people and do their best work then; others are better later in the day; and some discover that coming upon the midnight clear is for them. In contrast, you probably have a portion of the day when your attention and ability to concentrate are weak, so try to plan your leisure for your naturally slack periods. With me it's 4–6 p.m.

Using those odd bits of left over time can benefit you a lot
There are lots of small periods of time in the day that seem too short to start something new. They might be ten minutes or more in length and can arise at any time, e.g., waiting for a meal or sitting around after you've eaten, waiting for a train, travelling by bus, or filling in the gap before the next lecture.

These incredibly useful time slots are too often wasted. You can use them profitably for:
- Reading the notes you took earlier in the day.
- Reading your condensed notes from something studied earlier in the term.
- Planning an answer to a question in your textbook.
- Looking at an existing skeleton outline and trying to improve it.
- Maybe going through vocabulary flash cards if you are studying a language.

Finding a good place to study
Work out where you study best and try to get there. Some people like a clean desk with nothing on it but the notes they are using while others like clutter; some like sitting in an armchair with stuff piled around; others concentrate best when lying on the floor. You might like total quiet, or find you do better with background music playing as you baroque around the clock, unless of course you have Van Gogh's ear for music. You might find that choosing an unusual place to do this is particularly beneficial and helps you remember – try leaning against the front door, sitting on a (strong!) coffee table, or sprawling in the hallway. Whatever! If you find it works for you, go for it. Try not to make the requirements too stringent however, or they can seriously limit your ability to study.

☺ For those studying statistics, you should be aware that 64.7% of stats ☺ are made up on the spot – just like this one.

Practising questions from textbooks and study guides
Many textbooks include questions at the end of each chapter that provide you with the opportunity to practise preparing answers. If a study guide accompanies your textbook it, too, is a good source of questions. Never waste time writing out your answer in full unless you wish to practise your writing skills, but instead make a skeleton outline and put the question at the top.

Read the question carefully and think about it. Does it naturally divide into sections? If so, put these down and you have a start on your outline. You could then add what you can remember about the topic. After that put down what you personally think. You might then like to read the relevant bit of the textbook and expand your outline. Later in the term you can add even more – see "Gathering the information", page 79.

Don't worry if early in the term you cannot answer some textbook questions, as you will probably cover the material later in class. Keep your skeleton answers and file them with your notes on the topic – they make excellent revision material.

Practising answers in this way not only reinforces your knowledge and helps you to learn, it also develops a skill that will last you for life. In the exam room you will need to plan answers quickly; and after you leave university the same ability will enable you to devise fast logical responses to problems at work.

Oldies but goodies: going over old exam papers
Try to get hold of old exam papers – some universities sell them but you might find the library holds a full set anyway. Just like textbook questions, you can use these to sketch out your answers. You can also try to spot hot topics that come up more often than others, and concentrate your studies slightly more in those areas. Do not totally neglect areas that have not been asked about recently – there is always a first time! You may also need the information that does not come up much in first-year exams in your second or third-year.

He can't mean it, surely?
When an essay comes back, resist the urge to look up the mark and then file the paper away. The comments you get, either in the margin or at the end, are far more valuable to you than a mere mark – they show you where you can improve. When you have had a few essays back, it's a good idea to sit and look over all the comments; if you find you are getting similar remarks, it tells you that here is an area to concentrate upon. Check the comments you get against the list of common mistakes in Chapter 7, "Essay tips – a list of things to avoid", page 102. If you receive a comment that you don't understand, make an appointment to see the marker and politely ask him or her what it means and how can they help you improve. Most staff are happy to assist you if approached nicely.

Stop when you are genuinely tired
Death is nature's way of telling you to slow down, and maybe tiredness is an early warning signal. If you are studying and suddenly find you are falling asleep, stop and take a break of at least 15 minutes. Remember, you are trying to maximise your learning not the quantity of time expended. During your break, use one of the relaxation techniques (see the section on coping with nerves, page 91) or take a snooze if necessary. Chill out for a bit but remember to go back to studying afterwards!

Avoiding lunchtime drinking
Alcohol at lunchtime might seem attractive but it lowers your productivity and tends to make you sleepy when you are trying to study. Save your drinking for the evening if you can.

REMEMBER: A STUDY-BUDDY OR STUDY-GROUP IS THE MAGIC SECRET!

Working with a good study-buddy or group is the fast track to learning.

Things to do with your study-buddy (no, not that!)
- Compare and discuss your notes from the same lecture.
- Explain the main points of the lecture to each other.
- Go through the details of the lecture and see how they fit together.
- Before a lecture talk over what you think it will cover (read the assigned textbook chapter first).
- Read the same section of the textbook and explain it to each other or quiz each other on it.
- Take opposing views on any questions set for discussion, or papers you have to write, and argue.
- Pool the information you have each discovered about an assignment and discuss possible approaches.
- Share the photocopying costs of material you need.
- Revise jointly for exams, and test each other.
- Compare your skeleton outlines to the same answer.
- And if you are really into saving money, you could cut each other's hair for free. (Well, maybe not!)

Do all this and you too could be a high flyer.

Study-group therapy
A study-group is comprised of about three to six people who get together to cooperate and learn more easily, quickly and enjoyably. Such a group

can be fun, and immensely useful in helping you learn. You will find that it really is better with a little help from your friends.

Setting up the group
If you can, it is easier to join an existing group. If not, you can set up your own by asking a few people on the course who seem interested. It is best to do this personally because advertising on a board will probably not work: you might feel foolish; you may be criticised as a nerd by some of the heartier brethren knocking about the place; and the chances are you will attract some people you cannot work with and maybe wouldn't even wish to be seen hanging around with.

Try rotating the leadership
With a small group you may not need a formal leader, and can just meet and work together when convenient. Yet there is benefit in having a leader. It makes more efficient use of the limited time – people know when to meet, why they are there, and what they will do with the session. This allows them to prepare in advance. If you rotate the leadership, everyone gets a chance to learn skills (organising; persuading; motivating; group dynamics etc.) and you can put this on your Curriculum Vitae (CV or *résumé*) which will help you when you are looking for your first job. Employers are impressed by such things, and it gives you something valuable to talk about at the interview. Rotating the leadership also prevents one person from dominating too much.

☺   As every sledge dog knows, only the leader gets a change of view.   ☺

Learning with your study-group
You can do everything you can do with your study-buddy, and more. You can:

- Share the cost of textbooks – you each need the basic one but supplementary texts and other useful books can be bought and circulated within the group.
- Share the cost of articles downloaded from the Internet.
- Search for information by dividing up, so that each member can research into a part (or all) of the tutorial or seminar question and report back.
- Find more material by searching a greater number of journals and Internet sites.

- Once you have information you can brainstorm ideas about the answer. This is jargon for sitting around, throwing out suggestions, and discussing it from various angles.
- Later on you might engage in one or more group projects and will have a ready-made team that is used to working together.

Let us play: here are a few learning games for the group
- Who can recall the most from the recent lecture or last week's lecture? One minute (?) each.
- Who can say the most about a particular topic in the course? Two minutes (?) each.
- Choose a question – one person argues the case for, another the case against, for five minutes – then the group discusses it.
- Take a question and go round in turn, everyone having to say something about it.
- Take a question, set a time limit for thinking in which each person makes a skeleton answer; these are circulated, discussed and maybe an excellent composite answer made; then everybody gets a copy of this.
- Divide into two teams and argue the case for and against a proposition or question – this takes longer and may need half an hour or more.

Note: If you work on an assignment with others, it's best to restrict it to searching for information and discussions. It is wise not to plot out a detailed answer together because if you do it might lead to a subsequent charge of plagiarism should the individual essays look much alike. I once had to chair a committee investigating just such a case; after a lengthy and difficult meeting we finally acquitted the three students. We decided that it was not plagiarism and we could not penalise good study practice.

☺ If you're in a group, you're in the loop! ☺

GETTING TO GRIPS WITH THE SET TEXTBOOK

Buying your main text
You generally need to own a copy of the main set textbook but you can often buy one second-hand which will be cheaper. Check the notice-boards. Make sure you get the current edition, otherwise any page and

chapter references supplied in lectures will not fit. Buy a study guide too if there is one and work through it on your own, with your study-buddy, or in your group. A study-group can share the cost of a guide by buying perhaps only one for every two or three people.

If there is a computer disc that comes with the textbook and you have ready access to a machine, it is very helpful to work through the program. It provides useful self-paced learning and lets you steadily revise material covered earlier. The computer program also lets you see another version of the material and probably has exercises to reinforce what you are learning. You might find it helps to put a couple of slots into your weekly timetable to do this. It can also provide material for your study-group.

Book lists – in this case length does make a difference
You do not usually need to buy everything on the list. Some items will be good for only a small part of your course, while others may be out of date and no one has bothered to remove them. You may be able to use the library copies until you are certain what you need to buy. When you are presented with a long list, you might start by reading the most recent item on it, because it will have fewer out-of-date theories and probably contain more recent information.

☺ Studying = building small rooms in houses to put a desk in. ☺

Highlighting the highlights
It is usually not the best use of your time to take notes from your set textbook. It is better to highlight it and read those bits often. If as a child you were taught it was a crime to write in books – forget it! With few exceptions, a book is not a unique work of art and the bookshop will be more than happy to sell you dozens of identical copies if you wish. The only thing against highlighting is that it reduces the second-hand value of the book should you wish to sell it later. Yet keep in mind that your goal is to learn quickly and easily, not to maximise the value of old books. When highlighting, be careful not to go through marking everything, for there is no point. If you read the chapter or section through carefully first, it reduces the temptation to highlight the lot.

Choosing "the best" textbook
The textbook was set because someone thought it was generally the most suitable for that course. However, you might find that it is difficult to learn from, perhaps because it is dry, dull as ditch water and mega-boring; or perhaps it simply does not fit your personality well. You should try other textbooks in the library to see if they explain things in a way that you

understand better. To help you find a different text that suits you, look up your textbook in the library catalogue and locate it on the shelf, then examine the books around it. Look up an issue that you know a bit about and see how each book covers it. The book that you find the easiest to understand is the one for you. You can also ask in your study-group what others think about different textbooks – and swap books around too. Be aware that the staff are often not a good source of information on textbooks because they do not know what particular difficulties you face, nor are they in the habit of sitting and reading basic textbooks. I know of what I speak!

Finding what you need to know
When you have a whole topic you want to learn about, start by examining the contents page – there might be a whole section or even a chapter about it. If your need is more specific, it's often best to go straight to the index at the back and look it up. If you find several references, start with those with a range (e.g., "pp. 56-64") which is likely to deal with it in detail, whereas a lone "p. 12" may be just a passing reference.

EXTRACTING INFORMATION FROM JOURNALS

Should I photocopy it or take notes?
Read the article through before making a decision to photocopy. If there is much that you need, and perhaps tables of data, a photocopy might be a good idea. If you only need a small part of the article then taking notes is a cheaper and better option. Extracting the bits you want and writing them out also helps you to remember them.

You've paid for the photocopy: now read it!
Possessing a photocopy or carrying it around with you does not improve your learning in any way. You have to read it, you should highlight (or underline) the relevant parts, and ought to remember what is in it. Otherwise you have wasted your money.

Colour coding
Some students find it helpful to use, say, yellow paper for the notes taken privately from journal articles, books etc., and ordinary white paper for notes taken from formal lectures and the like. This can be of value if when revising you can force yourself to read a bit further than you otherwise

would and "finish the yellow pages too", but many find the whole thing more trouble than it is worth.

File your notes by topic
It usually works best to file your notes (whatever their source) by topic so that you can look up or revise easily. However, many students seem to find keeping their main lecture notes separately works for them; try it and see which you prefer.

BET YOU CAN IMPROVE YOUR READING!

Reading is like driving: many can do it, but few do it all that well. Most children are taught to read (literacy) but few are taught to read properly (efficiency). Unless you have already attended special courses, you should assume you do not read as well as you might. When reading for study purposes you need a pen and paper to hand. As you read, an idea might pop into your head. Ideas are valuable currency at university and you cannot afford to forget any, so write them down at once. The habit is useful for developing your ability to think and criticise in general.

Using different approaches to reading
The "Intro-Conclusion" approach is useful with journal articles. It often helps if you first read the introduction, then jump to the conclusion to get the gist of the paper – then go back and start to read it properly. This helps to focus the brain on the issue.

The approach of "SQ3R"
The SQ3R sequence approach is useful for larger texts and involves five stages:

Survey. You first skim through, reading the title, introduction and conclusion and the headings and sub-headings and anything in upper case, bold or italic print. This gives you an idea of what will be covered and imprints the main themes.

Question. You next think up a few questions on each section that you hope will be answered when you read it through properly.

Read. You then read it section by section and at the same time you look for answers to your questions.

Recall (or Recite). This means you close the book and try to think of the main points, perhaps jotting them down on a piece of paper. Say them aloud if it helps – this reinforces your memory.

Review. The last stage consists of going through the text more slowly and making your notes, adding to those from the recall stage or making new ones if necessary.

This method may seem slow and cumbersome but it sure makes most people remember what they read! It is a good idea to try this SQ3R way for a few weeks to see if it works for you, and if so stick with it. Note that it is important not to try out a new system once, decide that it is too time-consuming and tedious, and then give up on it. All new systems take a little getting used to, especially this one.

Don't leap in and start to take your notes
It's a good idea to read through the material before you start to take notes, otherwise you might end up noting the less important points or even copying out nearly the whole thing – a total waste of your time!

Speed reading
"Speed reading" is actually a misnomer: it can teach you to read more quickly, but an unexpected benefit is that it allows you to remember more of what you read. In addition, it teaches you to read different things more efficiently, which saves you even more time.

☺ I did a speed reading course and then read *Moby Dick* in five minutes ☺
– it's about a whale.

If your university offers a free course it is worth doing, but many commercial courses seem over-priced. Speed reading programs are now available for computers and provide a decent and cheaper alternative as long as you persist and practise. I found "Ace Reader" from Stepware Inc. particularly useful, and I confess that I rather enjoyed the little games.

Efficient reading
If you read efficiently you ought to read different things at different speeds because you are reading for different purposes. For this reason, do not be concerned if the textbook seems painfully slow going.

The following reading material can usefully be tackled at different reading speeds:
- Newspapers – you may only glance at the headlines, scan quite a lot of articles quickly but read only a few items properly.
- Escapist paperbacks – you can read these rapidly.
- Good novels – you might wish to read them relatively slowly.
- Textbooks and technical works – should be read the slowest of all.

Some tips that might help you to read more quickly
- When you pick up anything to read, ask yourself at what speed you should read – flat out, medium paced, or slowly. With a newspaper or magazine, run your eye down the middle of the column, trying to understand the content.
- Try to read in small chunks, of a few words or phrases, and do not look at each word as a separate item.
- The first time you start to read a journal article, try reading only the first sentence of each paragraph until you reach the end; then return to the start and read properly.
- Alternatively, read the first and last sentences of each paragraph.
- Even better, use SQ3R if you can.

☺ As all vet students know, one good churn deserves an udder.   ☺

THERE'S SOMETHING OUT THERE: OR HOW TO MAKE USE OF RESOURCES

Learning to use the library better
In recent years there has been rapid technological change in libraries so that computers are now widely in place. You need computer skills to use the catalogue and other information sources, and it is easier to find material than it once was. You should go to any course that your university holds on library use, pick up any pamphlets they have, and never be afraid to ask for help. Few new students can use a large library well and the sooner you gain the skill, the better.

In the first week of term, apart from making friends, you can look up the call numbers for the textbooks in your course (these are the numbers printed on the spine of the book) and go and see where they are located so you can find them again easily. You can add the call numbers to your reading list too, which will make your life easier in the future.

Remember that if you are searching the catalogue for material and the computer crashes, you can check the printed card catalogue that many libraries still keep. It is better than fuming and wasting your time.

Finding those useful but hidden library sections
Markers get so bored reading virtually identical answers to a question that if you can get in something a bit different but still relevant, they are so pleased they tend to be more generous with marks. Newer data, a different diagram or a fresh example can make your assignment stand out and help you gain marks. So where can you look?

The reference section
This is a collection of basic information that is often overlooked. It is worth browsing the shelves for an hour in the first week to see what your library holds. Make a note of the title and call number of anything that looks interesting and relevant to your course. You can use these items later for researching essays.

Electronic databases: searching library catalogues
Ask what electronic databases (other than the catalogue) are available in the library and what is on CD-ROM that you can use. Some newspaper, magazine and journal articles are now being put on discs. They can be a great source of recent information, but you often have to book in advance to use them. Some libraries also have computer access to other libraries or sources of information – ask at the help desk what is available and for any information on using them.

Searching electronically is something of an art, and the more you do it, the better you get. You often have to guess what phrases to search for. Some people try individual words – it saves time if you think up a list in advance. For instance, if you wish to know about vegetation growth, you might think of words like "trees", "shrubs", and "hedges"; then "irrigation" and "soil"; and finally, "manure", "fertiliser", "insecticides", and "pesticides". Note that some programs insist you check the singular as well as the plural, e.g. "tree" and "trees", while others are happy with the singular.

Phrases in inverted commas are a good way of narrowing your search; "plant growth" searches for that phrase only (over 11 million Internet hits, I just tried), whereas " 'plant growth' Europe" limits it to the same phrase *and* the word Europe (which narrowed it down to around half a million hits). If you learn a little Boolean logic (Google this to learn more) you can get even better at narrowing searches.

The government documents section
This is where you can expect government documents, including foreign government and United Nations material, to be stored. Often ignored by first-year students, this section can provide useful and original information that helps your work to stand out.

☺   Why isn't "phonetic" spelled the way it sounds?   ☺

Trying the Internet for extra information
Your university may give you free access to the Internet, but if not it can be slow and expensive unless you personally have broadband.

Your local authority library may provide good resources, including free Internet access
Some local authorities pay for subscriptions to sources like the *Encyclopaedia Britannica* and allow their residents to access these online at zero cost. Check out the public library in your university's area as well as your home town and see if you can get a library card to use these extra research sources.

Internet sources of useful information
- Newsgroups – tens of thousands in 2007 and still growing – where people swap ideas and information (often scurrilous and rude).
- Online libraries and document repositories (but often you have to pay to read the entire article unless your library has an account).
- Online search engines – there are several, but well-known ones include Google, Lycos, and Yahoo; there are also meta-search engines, that search several other engines at once, including Copernic Agent, Surfwax, and the splendidly-named Dogpile.

The Internet is in a constant state of flux, everything keeps altering, home pages and newsgroups move, and new sites come on as old ones disappear. You could check out a recent Internet magazine for a list of what might be useful to you and write down their Internet addresses or URLs (Uniform Resource Locator, but who remembers?). See Appendix A for a list of currently valid sites that I find useful.

The value of the Internet
It is a valuable source of information, is great fun, but it can be a sink down which you pour your precious time. You should think in terms of spending hours not minutes. Currently the information you can find varies in quality, and newsgroups are frequently the haunt of the interested but ignorant, so that you often get relatively few gold nuggets in return for a lot of digging. Use the information you find cautiously: if it is from a well-known source (such as a government or a United Nations agency) the data or other information is as good as they can get it. However, if it is from unknown names, the information can be misleading or totally incorrect – one never knows for sure! Apart from the sheer enjoyment involved, an important benefit of using the Net is that you will develop skills that can help you when seeking a job and developing your career.

☺   Campus = a gay cat.   ☺

CASE STUDIES

Aziz's motivation reaps results
Aziz is determined to succeed and sees his future in banking or perhaps insurance. His drive has led him to set up a study-group that meets regularly twice a week. He tends to dominate it a bit but he and the others find it most helpful. He is also enjoying university and in the evening he tells his partner what he did during the day – frankly, she is getting a bit bored with this but has put up with it so far and feels he is not yet turning into a grumpy old man.

Betty finds a study-buddy
Betty was worried that she was not learning much in tutorials and talked to the university adviser who suggested she find a study-buddy, which she has now done. She is not yet confident enough to join a group. She learns a lot studying on her own but finds discussing with her buddy reinforces her knowledge and occasionally he comes up with an idea that surprises her. She is enjoying university life more, is starting to build up her confidence and is learning well. She is still shy though. The study-buddy joins her for Friday lunch and she likes this. Will he turn into a boy friend?

Charlie is beginning to discover that going it alone can be tough
Charlie never thinks about a study-buddy or group learning and just turns up for some, but certainly not all, of the formal sessions. He is learning a bit but not much. On the plus side, he is having a really good time. He is now a borderline failure case and has become dimly aware of it, but he vaguely hopes somehow he will manage to do better and muddle through. He bats away the occasional depressing thought by thinking of the next party he will go to.

DISCUSSION POINTS

1. How many ways of using short periods of study time (say, up to half an hour) can you think of for your particular course or subjects?

2. What sort of learning game can you invent for an informal study group? (When you join such a group you can set this as a task for all.)

3. Where exactly can you find questions in your subjects for you and your study-buddy to practise answering?

SUMMARY

- Go over some of your old notes regularly, preferably each day.
- Explaining your notes to another is an excellent way of learning.
- Condensing your notes is also valuable.
- Take advantage of short periods of time and do not waste them.
- Practise planning a skeleton answer to one or two questions each day. You can file them with your notes on the topic.
- Pay more attention to the comments on your essays than the mark you get.
- A study-buddy will help you learn more quickly and make it fun.
- A study-group allows you to play various games that will improve your performance in an enjoyable way.
- You must buy the set textbook and should use it wisely.
- Try to read different types of material at different speeds.
- The SQ3R approach often helps: it means Survey – Question – Read – Recall/Recite – Review.
- Learn how to use your library's computerised databases.
- The Internet is a valuable source but can take up a lot of time for relatively little return. However, it remains an essential part of finding information.

4. Teaching, now that'll larn you

You really should go to all the set teaching sessions and not be tempted to miss out. Remember the problem of building a wall? Once you start missing blocks, it gets harder to build solidly on the increasingly shaky early levels. In addition, when you suddenly can't understand something, your motivation to study and succeed can easily start to evaporate. Only if you find some lecturer is truly hopeless, would you be better off skipping his or her lectures. If you make the decision to skip a lecture course, make sure you study the subject on your own in that period.

LECTURES – THE COURSE STARTS HERE

The teaching methods at university are usually different from those you had at school and you may have to learn a few new tricks.

Ah! Hand me the handout
Many lecturers provide course outlines, including lecture schedules containing recommended reading.

☹ There are handouts – ☺
and then there are handouts.

If your lecturer does not do this, a note asking if he or she would do so, with a little flattery about helping you to follow the excellent lectures, might pay off. Once you have a course handout, read it over regularly and get the "shape" of the course in your mind. Whenever a new topic is begun in the lectures, check the handout to see how far you have got and how it fits in. Seeing where you are going and where you have been seems to make learning easier for a lot of people.

Some lecturers provide an outline of each lecture as they begin; if yours does this, use it to clarify the organisation of the lecture. You still have to take your own notes – the outline will be insufficient on its own. As the course proceeds, if you get extra handouts (other than lecture outlines) this is prime information that you are expected to know. Read such handouts regularly and memorise them.

Psyching yourself up before the lecture – I can! I really can! And I want to!
If your course handout tells you what part of the textbook to read for each lecture, try to do this before the lecture is given. It will help you to follow the lecture as well as understand and remember the content more easily. Before the lecture you might find the time to review this material with your study-buddy and tell each other what the textbook meant; this is a very effective way of learning. It will also reveal any weak points in your understanding and may provoke questions, which you can ask in the lecture hall, if this is encouraged. On the way to the lecture, it will help you if you go over in your mind what was in the assigned reading and consider which bits the lecturer might focus on. This mental tuning up can help you. This is best-advice and OK, you might not do it all the time! Whatever turns you on... and it's no biggy.

Be comfortable!
Get there early and decide where to sit at ease before the lecture begins – you need to hear easily and see the board. Many students sit in roughly the same place each week as it makes them feel relaxed and comfortable. Once you are settled, psych yourself up if you did not do this on the way in. You can try to feel positive about how interesting the lecture will be, and ask yourself things like: will it follow the textbook, will it contradict it, or will the questions you thought up be answered? Hit those negative feelings of boredom or dislike on the head and be positive!

Messing around can mess you around big time
If you are going to sit there for an hour, you might as well get the most out of it. Sitting daydreaming in a university lecture is a total waste of your time. Once the lecture starts you should avoid chatting with the people around you. If you want to discuss last night's TV show, go outside and do it. No one forces you to be at the lecture, it is merely in your interest to be there and pay attention. Also, avoid giggling with friends, which disrupts the lecture and prevents other students from concentrating. If

you find your attention wandering in lectures, try to bring your mind back; perhaps you could think briefly about the job you want after you graduate (in order to raise the level of your motivation), or glance over the lecture outline if you have one, then settle down to concentrating again. Do not be overly concerned if this mind-wandering happens to you now and then (you're human, just like the rest of us) but do fight it.

Taking good notes

What do you need?
You will need to buy a cheap lined pad (a margin is useful for your comments and holes to use when filing) and the A4 size is best. A ring folder is essential. If you have to stand up to take notes (unlikely unless you do field work) you might find a clipboard handy. You will need one or two different coloured pens, or a multi-coloured one. Really cheap ball point pens tend to blob and smear so it is worth paying a little extra to get better ones. If it saves you ruining one shirt or blouse you are ahead of the game. A transparent plastic ruler can be handy, but only a few specific courses need a set-square. You might find a pencil useful for copying diagrams – if you make a mistake, rub it out. You can ink the diagram in later.

☺   Taking notes = robbing banks; but making notes = forgery.   ☺

Start slowly and only buy things when you really need them. Ultimately you might find you need a stapler, paper clips, correction fluid, several different coloured pens, some overhead transparencies, special overhead transparency pens in perhaps three different colours, scissors, adhesive tape, maybe a hole punch, and a cheap calculator.

Notes don't have to be noteworthy, just functional
At the top you should put the lecture topic, date, and lecturer's name – it can be useful later on to know where you got the information. You should only write on one side of the page if you can afford it because this makes it much easier to find things later. When your notes are in a ring folder, it means you have a blank left-hand page for your comments, ideas and other additions you might want to make; it is also easier to slot new notes in the proper place.

Listening for what's important
The lecturer will have first made a framework of what he or she wants to cover, in some logical order, and then he or she pads it out into words. Some prefer to read out from a script, others just use their framework and talk to it. Your task is to extract that framework and the main points within it; do not write down everything that is said, especially jokes and asides. Try to listen rather than write verbatim and make sure you come away with not only the main points, but also any criticisms of the textbook or a particular person's views, and get all diagrams, figures, tables, and references supplied. If you leave a lecture not knowing what it was about you might be writing down too much – read over the notes you took and see. Compare them with your study-buddy or group member if you like.

Clearly, you have to write
Make your notes legible and clear. It is tempting, but wrong, to save money by squashing up your writing – try not to be stingy with paper and leave plenty of room for your comments. If you make your notes a pleasure to look at and not all cramped up, you will read them more often and learn the content more easily.

Lay out your notes logically in clear handwriting, using one or two different colours if you wish. It is sensible to go through after the lecture and underline headings and important points in different colours, rather than do this at the time. The use of colour helps the important things to stand out and makes visual recall easier. If you read your notes often enough, you can get to picture them in your mind.

When taking notes you should always use abbreviations and symbols where you can. Many already exist and you can create your own – see Figure 3.

☺   Advanced algebra = a weapon of math destruction.   ☺

Don't waste time redoing your lecture notes
It is generally useless to laboriously copy out your notes again. It is of little value in helping you to remember them, and a better use of your time is to reread them, and then discuss them or explain the issues and concepts involved to others.

Figure 3. Some useful abbreviations and symbols you can use

asap.	as soon as possible	≠	not the same as
cf.	compared with	≡	identical to
do.	ditto; the same	↑	increases
eg.	as an example	↓	decreases
inc.	including	→	leads to
misc.	miscellaneous	Δ	changes

Note taking techniques
Using the dot-dash method of note taking can be very handy – this is the way it works:

<u>THE MAIN HEADINGS (at the left margin) ARE UNDERLINED, PERHAPS IN BLOCK CAPITALS</u> (like this).

- Minor headings are inset about a centimetre with a dot in front of the first word.

    – Sub-heads are inset again, with a dash in front.

        • Sub-sub-heads then get inset with a dot.

            – ... and so on.

You might wish to replace the dots and dashes with numbers later, if you think that seeing them as you revise will help you to remember the content.

The pattern method (see Figure 4, page 67)
This is a free form method of note taking which can be particularly effective when you are in a wide-ranging discussion that jumps about a lot. If you spread out the headings and leave plenty of space, you can return to any particular bit of the issue and add any extra points as they

emerge. You can also easily show interlinks between the points, one-way or two-way, using arrows.

Whoosh! Splat! Hey I missed that point completely!
You are likely to have an occasional problem of not understanding something in a lecture and as a statement flies past you, what can you do?

- Some universities allow questions: if yours does this, raise your hand – if you are not noticed, cough loudly; that'll get attention!
- Some lecturers deliberately leave time for questions at the end – ask then.
- Some will stay back to answer questions after the hour is up: ditto.
- You can make an appointment to ask the lecturer about it later that day or week. Remember to take your actual notes with you with the place marked so you can find it easily. Some academics have set "Office Hours" when you can simply turn up with questions.
- Discuss the question with your study-buddy or study-group – this might be the easiest way as somebody probably heard and understood it.
- Look up the textbook to see if the point is covered there.
- Look the point up in a different textbook.
- Ask a different tutor or lecturer about it.
- Listen to the tape of the lecture you or your university made, if one exists.

Taping the lectures
Some universities tape the first-year lectures and put them in the library. Check to see if yours does this. If not, you might find it useful to tape the lecture yourself. It is polite to ask permission of the lecturer in the theatre the first time you do it and thank them. After that, a nice smile will usually suffice as you put the machine down.

Figure 4. The pattern method of note taking

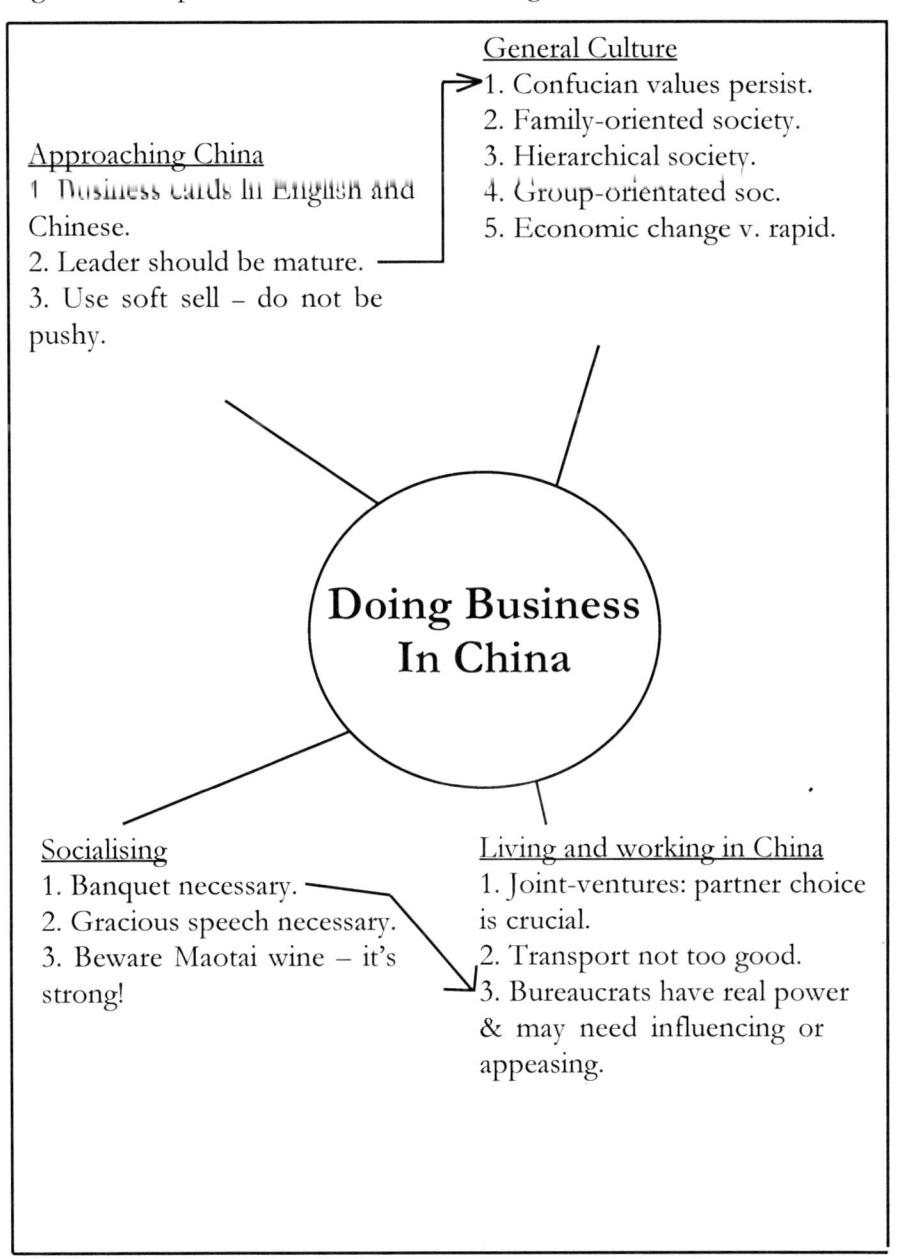

```
                              General Culture
                              1. Confucian values persist.
                              2. Family-oriented society.
   Approaching China          3. Hierarchical society.
   1. Business cards in English and   4. Group-orientated soc.
   Chinese.                   5. Economic change v. rapid.
   2. Leader should be mature.
   3. Use soft sell – do not be
   pushy.

                    ┌─────────────────┐
                    │  Doing Business │
                    │    In China     │
                    └─────────────────┘

   Socialising                Living and working in China
   1. Banquet necessary.      1. Joint-ventures: partner choice
   2. Gracious speech necessary.  is crucial.
   3. Beware Maotai wine – it's   2. Transport not too good.
   strong!                    3. Bureaucrats have real power
                              & may need influencing or
                              appeasing.
```

The benefits of taping lectures
If you missed a bit of the lecture – maybe you lost concentration briefly or someone had a coughing fit – you can check the tape to see what was

said. If you miss a lecture and use a tape to catch up, you might find it helps if you listen to the whole tape before you start taking notes. This assists you in sorting out the logical framework, and it will also help you to remember what was said because you hear it twice. But it takes twice as long.

The limitations of taping lectures
Listening to the official tape in the library is not a substitute for attending the lecture:
- Many lecturers write important concepts of the lecture on the board as they talk and you miss this valuable help unless you are there.
- You cannot see any diagrams, maps etc. that the lecturer may use.
- The tape can be fuzzy and indistinct, maybe with missing bits.
- Transcribing tapes is tedious and time-consuming.

And if you tape it yourself:
- The tape may run out before the end and you might have to rush up and turn it over. Embarrassing!
- If you attend and tape 3 hours of lectures you are likely to find it boring to listen to them yet again. And if you don't do this, unless you day-dream in lectures, why bother to tape?

☺   If you are ever asked to study Latin verbs – decline.   ☺

Taking lecture notes is only the start
In order to use the lecture notes to good effect and remember them more easily:
- Go over your notes relatively soon after the lecture – certainly the same day (early reinforcement).
- As you do this, you can add useful colours, underlines, and marginal comments (make the notes memorable).
- Compare your lecture notes with your study-buddy or group, discuss the issues, and explain the main points to each other. You might find you missed something important and it should make a lot more sense after the discussion (reinforces and improves the quality of your notes).
- A quick glance over your notes the next day and you should be well on the way to remembering the information.

TUTORIALS AND SEMINARS: GO IN AND WIN!

Preparing well beforehand
You need to do some work before you go to a tutorial or seminar: just turning up and hoping to get something out of the session is like going into battle unarmed. You should read whatever material was set and make a few notes about it, including any criticisms you have, and maybe an indication of what you think. After that, if you can find the time, it would help you to spend a few minutes discussing it with your study-buddy or group, but this is not essential. If no material was set, try looking up the general issue in a textbook anyway.

At the tutorial or seminar
In the session, you will listen to a paper, take a few notes, and ask questions at the end. The reading you did earlier, plus whatever you gleaned from the paper, should be enough to allow you to think up a question or two. If you ask the first (sensible) question it gets you noticed and you start to build up a reputation for ability.

Taking notes in tutorials and seminars
If the topic is new to you, you might wish to extract the paper's outline and main points, but if you already know something about the subject, just the new and interesting points and sources might be enough. To some extent it depends on your psychological make-up.

Don't be mute in the tute! Join in!
Do not sit like a pudding and let the discussion flow around you, but try to ask questions and participate. You will learn more about the subject that way and clarify your own ideas and position. You will also learn how to defend a view and, if necessary, to change your mind gracefully. This is a great place to learn such skills for the jobs you will have in the future.

Attending tutorials and seminars
You should always go to the tutorials and seminars, even if the title sounds boring. It may turn out to be better than you expect. In any case it will henceforth be assumed that you have both covered and understood the issue. Heck! Even if it doesn't seem immediately relevant, the information you get may be needed later in the course – and you can gain valuable skills from the process.

Oh no, it's my turn: presenting the paper (and see Chapter 6)
When you have to give a paper, although presenting in the first few weeks sounds alarming, choosing to go early in the term is often better, because:

- The markers may be more lenient as they know you have had little time to prepare and have only just begun the course.
- You also get one assignment out of the way and can then relax a bit.
- If you should fall ill and have to postpone delivering a paper, it is easier to reschedule if this is early in the term.
- Towards the end of the term, the exams are looming, long essays may be due, and you may start to feel stressed and short of time.
- If it is possible, it's a good idea to scatter your assignments over the first three quarters of the term and leave the last two or three weeks free for revision or any catching up sessions you have to do.

NO SWEAT IN THE WORKSHOPS AND LABS

Prepare in advance
There may well be preliminary set readings or exercises to do, depending on the nature of your subject. It is important you do these in advance so that you get the most out of the sessions. If you're going to be there, don't waste it!

In workshops, you need to get in and do things, participating as much as you can. You should avoid sitting back and coasting; the more you participate – entering into the debate, discussing alternatives, arguing against the set material or the views of others – the more you benefit. However, it is best not to present a silly view and argue it strongly just for effect, because this will annoy your fellow students.

You'll benefit if you take a few notes in your group work
As well as discussing, arguing, and using equipment at the time, you should take brief notes about what was done and said, or observations you made, as well as any tutor's comments. If you file these with the appropriate topic they can be useful for revision purposes.

CASE STUDIES

Aziz participates well
Aziz throws himself into tutorials and workshops and is beginning to be regarded as a leading light. He is so enthusiastic, the tutor has already had to restrain him in order to let the others have a turn but Aziz took this well. He really enjoys the workshops and looks forward to them. He gets a reasonable amount from lectures but he is not yet adept at extracting the main framework and is vaguely aware that he could do better here.

Betty gains most from lectures but least from the other sessions
Betty gets lots from lectures and psychs herself up by going over last week's notes, doing the set reading and thinking about it. Her main weakness is she has a tendency to write down everything that the lecturer says. She gets less from tutorials, and less again from workshops, where she is too shy to say anything and only sits and listens: just as Hamlet did, she chooses to "Give it an understanding, but no tongue". Right, she learns a bit from the general discussion but far less than she could if she had joined in. She understands that she needs to loosen up but finds it hard because she is essentially an introverted person.

Charlie is gaining little from lectures
Charlie just turns up to lectures, well maybe not all, but without any psyching up period so he is getting less from them than he could. He gets distracted easily and if he thinks of something interesting that is nothing to do with the lecture he tends to chat about it with one of his friends. On the other hand he gets more from the workshops, although again he does not prepare in advance. The reason he does better here is that he participates strongly – this is really because he enjoys talking with his mates, but as long as the discussion is on track he benefits. Against this, he has already missed a couple of lectures and tutorials and feels he is no worse off – wrongly!

DISCUSSION POINTS

1. Compare your notes with someone else's: what can you learn from each other about approach and layout?

2. Do you naturally enjoy questioning and arguing? If not, what could you do to help you to join in tutorial discussions?

3. How many ways can you think of for reviewing your notes after lectures and tutorials? Can you invent a game for two or more people to do this together?

SUMMARY

- You should go to all the set lectures, tutorials, workshops and lab sessions.
- Get hold of a syllabus or course outline and study it.
- Psych yourself up before each lecture, tutorial or workshop.
- Do not waste your time when in lectures and other meetings.
- Take good notes in formal sessions, especially in lectures.
- Do not rely solely on taped lectures.
- Go over your lecture notes the same day for early reinforcement.
- Do your tutorial papers early in the term if you can.
- Prepare something in advance for tutorials and workshops.
- Join in the discussion in tutorials and workshops and participate enthusiastically. Enjoy!

5. Information, information: how to organise and use it

When you study at university you will find your notes continually expand but they don't come in a strict logical order. It will make your life easier if you organise them so that you can quickly find what you want. When you come to prepare assignments if you can't find what you want, you might as well not have it.

WHERE THE HECK IS IT? FILING YOUR NOTES FOR EASY ACCESS

Your daily file
Most days you will find yourself making notes, and these are easily and safely carried in a ring binder or envelope file. It's a good idea to put your name and department on it, so that if you accidentally leave it somewhere, someone might hand it in and your valuable work will not have gone for good.

Your permanent files
With any filing system, good preparation is better than later perspiration. In your early days, ring binders are fine for your stock of notes at home. If you use one binder for each subject you can separate the notes into sections using tabbed dividers. Some students prefer box files instead but many might find these less convenient, as they are harder to organise internally and you might experience some difficulty in finding a particular item you want.

As your notes build up there is a cheap and good system available. Manila folders cost little and work well. Using a different coloured folder for each different subject helps a lot ("If it's blue it must be history"). You can keep adding new folders for each new part of a subject – a short title on the tab will identify it. It's better not to number them because their order is likely to change over time.

You do not need to buy a filing cabinet to keep the folders in: you can easily store your files in one or more cardboard boxes. Most local convenience stores are delighted if you want to take a few away but ask first; remember to take a folder with you to check the size of box you need. If you have an out-of-date folder that you wish to recycle it's easy; don't bother to reach for the correction fluid, but simply turn the folder inside out and lo! The tab and cover are clean again. If you ever need to do it a second time, you can then use the fluid or a gummed label.

Putting notes on a computer

Until recently, it was not really worth putting your notes on a computer or typing them up as it took time that could be better spent learning them. The only real exception to this was if your writing was so awful that even *you* would have trouble reading it later. However, technology progresses rapidly and things have changed a lot. Currently there is a choice between tablet PCs, digital pens, and voice-recognition software.

☺   Laptop = front of skirt, jeans, or trousers.   ☺

Tablet PCs advertise themselves for handwriting recognition but they vary a bit in their rate of success. That said, an expensive Toshiba model I have used was particularly adept at recognising my awful scrawl. It showed me what it thought I'd written (got it right every time!) and I then pasted it into my word processor. This particular machine also had voice-recognition software built in. Good stuff! But the screen was small, and generally they are still on the expensive side for many students.

A digital pen is cheaper and allows you to take notes that it stores automatically as you write. You can send the results to your mobile phone or download the notes into a PC, where handwriting recognition software translates them for your word processor. There is even a pen available for the Blackberry if you are wealthy enough to own one. You may need to train the computer to recognise your writing, but the results can be quite good. You will still have to check the notes for accuracy however.

Voice-recognition software is getting better and if you read slowly and carefully, using a program like *Dragon Naturally Speaking* or *ViaVoice*, you can put the notes taken in a lecture onto your PC. Again, training is necessary to improve the program's accuracy (you can expect over 95 per cent – which still leaves a fair number of errors), especially if you have a strong local accent. A quiet background improves your results, but if you want to really do well it is worth buying a good microphone.

I'VE REALLY GOT TO START THAT ASSIGNMENT

Every assignment you do goes through three stages
- You gather information and organise it.
- You read your notes, decide what you think, and plan out your answer.
- You write it up.

For good marks at university, the first two stages are the really important ones, although paradoxically many students tend to worry more about the final stage of writing. When you get the first two stages right, the essay almost writes itself. Discussing the issue with others can provide valuable assistance in preparing an assignment and can help you gain even better marks. Figure 5 illustrates the stages of preparing what could turn out to be a great assignment.

Making a start
Even if you have always wished to be a procrastinator but kept putting it off, that urgent assignment needs action. Just start! Pick up a pen and a piece of paper and begin jotting down things like:
- What you think about the topic.
- Why you think you were afraid to begin (this might show you what to tackle in the future).
- Any ideas on how it might be organised.
- Where you might find information about it.
- Any famous names that are associated with the topic so that you can quote them.
- Who you know that you could talk to about it.
- Any points that occur to you that are relevant to the question.
- And maybe a rough outline of a possible answer.

Figure 5. How to start an assignment

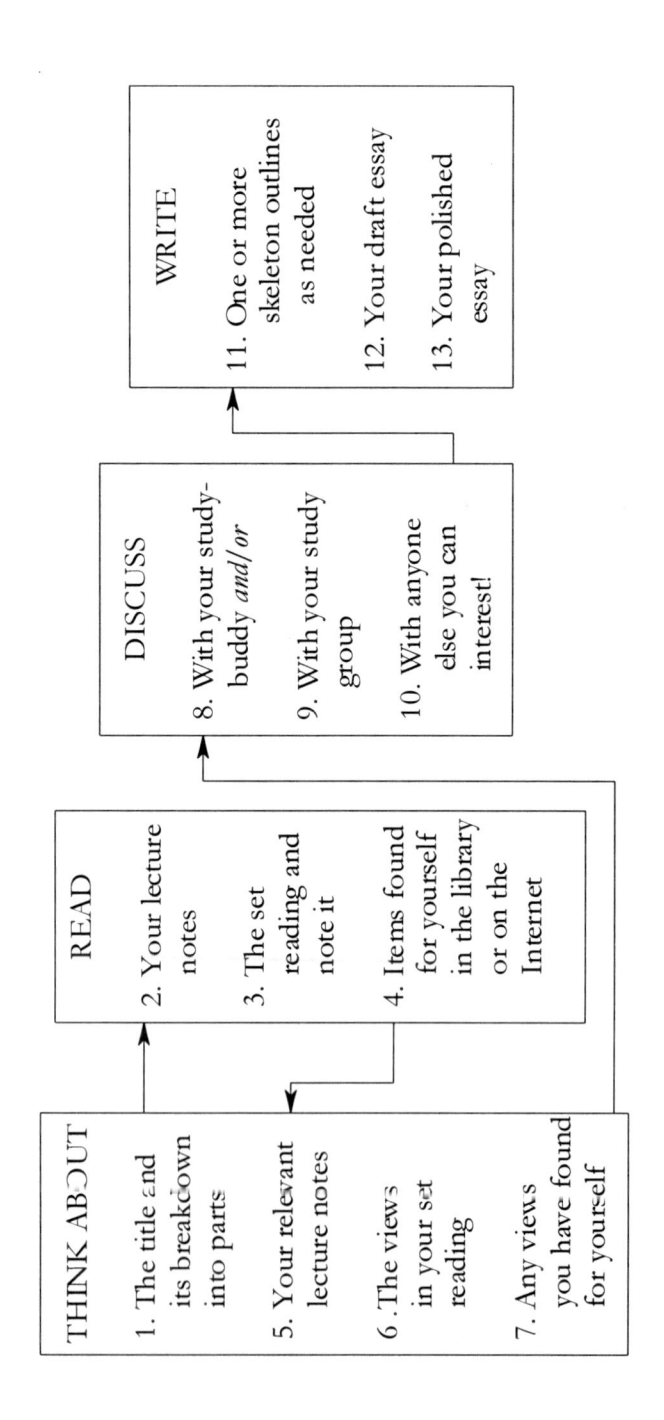

THINK ABOUT
1. The title and its breakdown into parts
5. Your relevant lecture notes
6. The views in your set reading
7. Any views you have found for yourself

READ
2. Your lecture notes
3. The set reading and note it
4. Items found for yourself in the library or on the Internet

DISCUSS
8. With your study-buddy *and/or*
9. With your study group
10. With anyone else you can interest!

WRITE
11. One or more skeleton outlines as needed
12. Your draft essay
13. Your polished essay

And if you still cannot make a start
- Talk to your study-buddy about the question or discuss it with your group.
- Promise yourself a reward when you have made your first outline answer – a nice cup of tea, a piece of chocolate, watching a (short!) piece of day-time TV... stuff like that.
- Set yourself a punishment if you don't start within half an hour: no sweets or ciggies for the next 4 hours, no alcohol before 7 p.m., or whatever. Or maybe you'll sweep or vacuum the carpet, wash up those grotty dishes, make the bed and tidy up all those clothes on the floor or draped over chairs.
- If it's really difficult to pick up that pen, set yourself both a reward and a punishment!

☺   Art students: does your heart belong to Dada?   ☺

Improving your mental attitude
Lay aside the list of ideas you have just made, take a break, and then return to it in about 20 minutes. Look it over, tell yourself the question is interesting, and persuade yourself that you look forward to finding out as much about it as you can (motivate and salivate!). Maybe picking up a book on the issue and reading the contents page might help. You should find your interest develops with such activity.

It is easy to feel too afraid to begin if the question seems big and difficult – it may look like mission impossible but isn't really! A big topic need not frighten you. All you have to do is to divide it into manageable sections or bite-sized pieces and keep nibbling away at it until it is done. Start with a simple outline and keep expanding it by dividing more and more finely. The project should seem easier when each separate part of your plan looks feasible.

Gathering the information
When you have begun thinking about the assignment in this way, what do you do next? It is always best to start with the easy and big, and then move later to the more difficult and small. You might follow these suggested stages:
- Start with your textbook – what does it have to say about the topic?
- Then use your lecture notes – anything of value there?
- Then move on to your notes from tutorials, seminars, workshops etc. – maybe you'll get lucky!

- About now you should go onto the Internet and search for information. There is a huge amount of information out there (but don't believe all you read!) and it can help to personalise your answer for a better mark. You might find the online Wikipedia (see Appendix A) worthwhile and if not, well, it's free. But be careful when consulting it – some people find it funny to put in misinformation just for laughs. Such items are removed as soon as they are found, but in the meantime... Your university library might also allow you free online access to resources such as journal articles that normally impose a charge for downloads.
- You can check if your local library allows free access to online resources that normally charge: mine allows me into the *Oxford Reference Online* amongst other goodies.
- Use the Uni library itself. Don't forget the encyclopaedias and "Dictionaries of..." relevant to your discipline – these can be good places to consult early. *The New Fontana Dictionary of Modern Thought* may be a good place to check if faced with a new idea or concept.
- It is a good idea to look up your lecturer's name in case he or she has published in that area – and you should list them in the bibliography if they have. If a well-known professor at your Uni has published about the issue then their name might well go in too.
- Then move on to other specialist books via the library catalogue if you need in-depth material.
- You might try the CD-ROMs in the library.
- Finally, you could search the journals for anything useful for your topic.

OK, it's a lot of recommendations: there's a good chance that you will not do all the above, especially the later stuff, but the more you find time for, the better mark you could get!

I'VE GOT LOTS OF INFORMATION – NOW WHAT?

Questions you might ask yourself
- What are the causes and effects?
- How does it work?
- What is the relative importance of each issue?
- Does it clash with other theories or data I have and how can I explain that?
- Are there any well-known names associated with different views about the question?
- What do I personally think about it?

Important ingredients in an assignment
- Structure: you will need an introduction, the main body of text, and a conclusion.
- The introduction must be consistent with your conclusion.
- A logical organisation for your information.
- Analyse it! Do not merely describe.
- Maintain a theme (if this is appropriate to the question).

Some recommended approaches
- Try putting only one idea in each paragraph.
- Try presenting the standard case before going on to make criticisms of it.

Recognising standard forms of questions
- Give the case for and against X and sum up (analysing and providing judgement).
- Compare and contrast two different theories or events (say where they are alike and where they differ).

- Estimate the effects of A on B (judging the importance of particular links and relationships).
- Estimate how much one or more things caused X (analysing and providing judgement plus the importance of links).
- Comment on a statement or quotation (rarely straightforward; requires explanation and judgement, possibly critical).
- Explain how X might affect... (can mean applying a model or some person's theory).

In almost every case the marker is looking for you to answer the question asked, and in doing so to present relevant points, organised in a logical fashion, and display the ability to reason by reaching a considered judgement based on the evidence you have presented. Simple facts are useful to bolster an idea but are mostly less important.

The following are some examples that don't do this and therefore often lead to poorer marks

- Describing what happened without analysing it.
- Using a straight chronological approach.
- Not answering the question that was asked, but drifting into a different one.
- Putting down everything you know about the issue rather than providing an answer ("The shotgun technique", page 103).
- Not using a theoretical model when one or more is available.

DECIDING WHAT YOU THINK: SUDDENLY IT GETS TRICKY!

Some points to be aware of

- Some of what you have been told and believe to be true is in fact untrue, or only partially true, but you do not know which bits.
- When someone disagrees with you, keep an open mind; they just might be right.
- What you think of as normal or reasonable behaviour may not be what others will think or do.

- You cannot rely on your own experience to determine what the truth is. You are a sample of one, which is always too small.
- Plausibility does not mean a thing is true.
- Consistency does not prove an argument is true.
- A larger number of supporters does not ensure the truth.
- The views of someone you like or trust need not be true.
- The latest information is not necessarily true (my experience of working with government officials indicates that they often seem to assume it is).
- The world is complex and we try to simplify our understanding of relationships by developing theories, and although he overstated the case, Oscar Wilde once pointed out that the truth is rarely pure and never simple.
- Despite this, you cannot assume that the more complex the argument, the more truth it must contain.
- Truth is best revealed by testing theories against the facts. As new theories and facts emerge, what we believe to be true gets refined and altered. That is one reason why history keeps getting rewritten.
- Different people can accept the same model or assumptions but still have different opinions or reach different conclusions if their priorities or values are not the same.
- If possible, reach a decision – but sometimes a definite "maybe" might be an acceptable answer.

Planning: the truth is in there

By now you have read a lot, made notes, and done some thinking; it's time to get down to it. When sketching out your preliminary approach, you can start by jotting down anything that springs immediately to mind. The pattern method of note taking (see Figure 4, page 67) allows you to organise your early ideas nicely, so you might try this. The skeleton approach is more logical and might be used at the second stage, because it helps you to get your ideas in a suitable order for writing. But whatever works best for you is cool!

Discussing the topic with others
Your study-buddy and study-group are your best options for discussion. If you have avoided developing either, then you will have to make use of any close friend. It is tempting to skip this stage but it really helps a lot. Brainstorming (sitting around throwing out spontaneous ideas, noting any

good ones, but without any organised agenda, thus generating alternative solutions) a topic in this way is valuable as it helps you to organise your thoughts and exposes any weak points before you write. You might get some new ideas too.

Assessing data reliability
Sometimes you will find conflicting views and evidence. What can you do to help choose between them?
- Ask yourself does the author have an axe to grind? (Political; national; religious; race; gender, age, social class...).
- Consider the author's likely ability. (Have you heard of him/her; who does s/he work for?)
- Who published the book or journal? (Are they respectable; are they well known?)

If no other considerations are involved you might prefer:
- UN data over national sources.
- National data over one institute's data.
- Official statistics over private ones.
- Statements by well-known authorities in the area.
- A work coming from a major publisher.
- Journals over magazines and especially over newspapers.
- Later data rather than earlier.
- Stuff published in hardcopy rather than merely found on the Internet (where lies and inventions abound).

Note: statements from such preferred sources are not necessarily better; but pragmatically they are easier for you to justify if challenged!

☺ Consider carefully if the evidence you found is partial and incomplete: ☺ some people use statistics and facts like a drunk uses a lamppost – more for support than for illumination.

It's all too much – what can I leave out?
When you have gathered sufficient information, you may have to decide what to discard. This is a good thing! It is the penalty of knowing a lot. One guide is to keep asking yourself if the particular point or piece of data is strictly relevant. You can do this by regularly going back to read the title of your essay or project and examining your entire outline to see if the point really does fit in and if so where does it look best.

How long should it be?
Students seem to ask this question every year. If you have been given a maximum number of words or a guide to length – fine. If not, then the real answer is "as long as it needs", which admittedly isn't a lot of help. You should ask your tutor or lecturer what sort of length is expected, or you could check with last year's students. As a very rough guide, for essays in many subjects, papers in the first-year might be three to eight typed pages long when double spaced, but check that your institution expects this and your particular course demands it. A term paper will be longer than a weekly one of course. Rarely is one A4 page enough, except perhaps in a subject like maths. But remember, if it's short it should be perfectly formed if you are to get a good mark. With oral papers, around 20 minutes might suffice as it allows time for questions and discussion.

Choose your own approach
The approach you adopt can also affect the length. Except in a few areas like maths, there is often no such thing as "the correct answer", only a choice of approaches. You often have to devise your own plan of attack and determine what boundaries you will put on the topic, drawing your own lines. In this, you must be sensible and always be prepared to defend the boundary lines and your approach. As a loose rule of thumb, in some subjects it pays to address a question from a theoretical point of view and use a model if appropriate. You can then present data and examples to justify what you are saying.

AVOIDING PLAGIARISM: DO YOU COPY, GOOD BUDDY?

Plagiarism means copying someone else's work and presenting it as your own. Despite the apparent advantages of theft over honest toil, it is a deadly sin at university; it is embarrassing if you are found out; and it is severely punished. If you are caught, a careful eye will be kept on you in future; your reputation will suffer; and you will find it harder to get a decent reference when seeking that first job. It also means you fail to develop useful skills and are unlikely to remember what you copied. Besides, do you want to be the only cat unanimously elected as a life member of the Cheetahs R Us society?

CASE STUDIES

Aziz doesn't prepare thoroughly enough
Aziz starts to prepare his first assignment but his enthusiasm causes him to skip ahead and he starts to write too early, relying on his ability to get him through. He has not yet investigated the library's CD-ROMs or free Internet sources. He is looking for a good mark but will feel a bit disappointed with his result.

Betty's good preparation leads to good marks
Betty prepares well. She invents several different skeleton answers and keeps adjusting the latest one as she finds more information – she uses the CD-ROM databases in the library and searches the Internet for information. She found Google Scholar of help although she had to pay for a copy of an article herself and has no study-group to split the cost with. She has also found a very useful UN survey of the field in the government section of the library.

Charlie pays the penalties of poor preparation
Charlie does little preparation and has not yet found his way around the library. He starts by writing down a few ideas but he doesn't develop a proper outline, and his poor mark reflects this. He does not read a newspaper, and current events tend to pass him by. He finds the writing part really difficult but the real reason is not a lack of writing skills. It is because he doesn't actually know what he wants to say.

DISCUSSION POINTS

1. In your subject, how many skeleton outlines would it be reasonable to devise for a question before you start to write it up? Would you rather discuss your outline with one person or with a group?

2. Where would you start looking for information about an assignment in your particular subjects? Where might you find relevant information in a place few others might think of looking?

3. If you have a major assignment to do and have been putting it off, what could you do to force yourself to start? Make a list and keep this – it might come in handy later!

SUMMARY

- File your notes by topic and in a way that helps you find them when needed.
- Never be afraid to start working on an assignment.
- Consider carefully how best to tackle the question – there is usually more than one way.
- You may have to decide between sources of different reliability.
- Design your own approach, draw your boundary lines, and be prepared to defend both.
- Copying other people's work might seem attractive but don't do it! It does not help you to develop the skills you will need later in life; and you will probably not remember that stuff for the exams either.

6. Orals are worth more than the paper they're written on

Orals are really something you can get your teeth into. However, for many people, the first time they have to deliver a paper out loud is at university and it can be a bit frightening. What is the best way to tackle an oral?

It's a good idea to write out your oral presentation like an essay and then read it aloud
This is easier, safer and almost always the best way in your first-year. In later years, some students try presenting an oral purely from notes: this is harder but develops your confidence, capacity to persuade, and skills in public speaking. See Chapter 10 for ways of developing your public speaking talents. Writing it out is probably best for most people, however. At the grad student level you should always write it out because the audience is often very critical and you might be asked to repeat the exact words you used earlier.

Think about the questions you might be asked after your presentation
Anticipating the sort of questions you may face can reduce your nervousness and allow you to perform better. It's worth considering possible questions at least a day before your presentation and work out some replies in advance. Knowing what you will say to a few obvious questions can put a warm safe glow under your belt.

The main types of questions you can expect
- Factual: "Did you say earlier that ...?"; "Did you find that...?"; "Did you consult...?"; "What did you mean by...".
- Expressing a view and asking what you think: "I think that...I would value your comments". (This one often opens up the discussion more widely.)

- Pointing out a weakness or missing elements: "Possibly you underrated [overestimated] the influence of..."; or "I saw no mention of...".(Be prepared to explain why you feel it less [more] significant etc.)
- Pointing to implications: "What you said about X, suggests that...".(This often involves explaining how it fits in with other events, conflicting theories, or alternative interpretations.)

Making handouts
In many courses a handout is not expected but in others it might be the norm or even be stipulated that you must give a handout to each student that attends. Even if you are not forced to do so, it might help you gain marks if you still prepare and pass out a piece of paper, as it can impress the staff member.

What could go on your handout?
- Your name and the topic title, together with the course and date.
- The name of the staff member, with their proper title (Professor or Dr if applicable – and check to make sure you spell their name right!)
- The outline of your talk.
- Any data or diagrams you will refer to or use in some way.

Handout tips
- Use both sides of the paper when you are photocopying to save money.
- Make sure there are no silly spelling errors or other mistakes.
- Do not make your handout an exact duplicate of an overhead transparency (OHT) that you intend to use.
- Keep it short. A long handout can cause people to look down while reading and this prevents you gaining eye contact when you want it.

DOING A DRY RUN

Consider holding a practice session the day before to read your paper aloud: this rehearsal allows you to see how long it takes and it will also help build your confidence. Read it out slowly at the speed you will adopt in the session – many people tend to talk too quickly in public, partly from nerves. If you discover that your paper is too long or too short you have time to adjust it. Often papers tend to be too long, especially when you have learned a lot about the topic. Ask your study-buddy or a friend to listen, time it, and watch you carefully. They can offer helpful critical comments about your voice and body language as well as the content of the paper. You can do the same for them when it's their turn.

COPING WITH NERVES – IT'S COOL TO HANG LOOSE

Relax! Or I'll creep up silently and suddenly jump out and punish you (OK, I lied)
Feeling nervous is normal and useful – you can use it to improve your motivation. Excessive fear, however, is not helpful, especially if you blank out temporarily and forget what you have learned. You might find it valuable to learn how to relax, not only for oral presentations but also before exams or interviews and in other times of personal stress. It can even help you to fall asleep at night. There are a number of different ways of relaxing and you might already be adept at one. If not, some techniques are presented here for you to try.

☺   If an audience comes in with great expectations, make sure you don't   ☺
    give them bleak house.

As part of their method, many relaxation techniques rely on slow breathing, filling the stomach first, before the upper lungs. Note that you should never simply take lots of really deep breaths to try to relax as it can be dangerous, causing you to hyperventilate. If you ignore this advice with the result that you start feeling weak, giddy, or faint, breathing in and out of a paper bag (never plastic) can help you to recover.

Which is the chilliest of the chill-outs?
If you want to see which way works best for you, try each of the following techniques – using a different one each day. Start by taking your pulse and make a note of the rate per minute. Then try one technique for maybe half an hour or so (whatever it takes) and afterwards immediately take your pulse again. Write it down and compare the two results and you will see how much your heart beat has slowed. After a few days, you can compare the results and see which technique slows your heart down the most – this is the most effective method for you. After a few weeks'

practice you will be even better at your chosen technique. Note that a full relaxation session might last for up to an hour (depending on how stressed you are), but even a few minutes are beneficial. Don't worry if you go under – it's rather like sleeping – then resurface later. This is normal and healthy. If at first you find you have a tendency to smile or giggle, ignore it. It is a defence mechanism – your subconscious mind may worry about this new event and try to reject it. Once it accepts the process as beneficial, your tendency to giggle should disappear.

If you can sit cross-legged or in the lotus position in comfort for a long period of time, that's great and you can do that while you relax. Otherwise it's fine to lie on a bed or on a thick rug on the floor, or you can even lounge back in a comfortable armchair.

☺   Time is the best teacher – unfortunately it kills all of its students.   ☺

Relaxation technique one: imagining a rural scene
You lie quietly on your back, arms by your side, palms up or down and with your fingers relaxed and slightly curled, or else in a comfortable chair with your arms on your thighs. Keep your eyes closed and consciously try to relax for ten seconds, breathing slowly. You now picture a peaceful rural scene (you drifting in a boat on a lake, sauntering down a country lane, sitting in a glade in a wood... whatever); try to include sounds, like birds singing, the breeze in the trees, or water trickling. Hold onto this calm, quiet picture and enjoy it.

Relaxation technique two: tackling the offending muscles
You lie down, sit etc. as above. Take your attention to your jaw and mouth and consciously slacken the muscles, letting your jaw sag. Do the same with your neck and shoulders, then fingers and toes. Continue going round the rest of your body for best results, then relax. A variation of the technique is first to tighten up a muscle group and hold it tense for five to ten seconds then let go suddenly. If you adopt this modification, it helps if you wait a few seconds before moving on to the next set of muscles.

Relaxation technique three: the simple breath approach (my favourite!)
You lie down, sit etc. as above, then:

Variation A. Take your attention to your toes and breathe in slowly, picturing and feeling your breath flowing over your feet, up your legs and over the top of your body to your head; as you breathe out, picture and feel your breath running down your back all the way to your heels. Keep it up for as long as you like – maybe one or two minutes if in an exam room and short of time or up to thirty minutes or so if at home.

Variation B. Picture the whole world around you as gleaming silvery white as you lie there; when you breathe in slowly the breath is bright and silvery; as you breathe out it is dark and gloomy as you expel toxins from the body. Timing as for A.

Variation C. If you can identify any particular pain, discomfort or weakness in any area of your body, imagine that the silvery breath is going into that target area and healing it or driving away the problem. As you breathe out, black sludgy stuff pours out of your skin and disappears into the ether.

> ☺ Is it because Shakespeare was afraid of walking cattle that he warned ☺
> us to beware the hides of march?

Relaxation technique four: the count-down
You lie, sit etc. as above. Choose a number – try something between 10 and 20 if under pressure in the exam room, 50-100 if at home. Each breath in-and-out will count for one. Starting with 20 as an example, breathe in slowly, thinking of the number and visualising it in your head, and breathe out. Then change to 19, visualising yourself moving down to it, and breathe in and out. Continue counting down to zero and stop. If you forget what number you are on it doesn't matter – just relax and go back to the last number you can remember. When you have had enough, count your breaths up from one to five, one breath at a time, before opening your eyes. You might find that you do not get anywhere near zero, especially once you have had some practice. That's good!

All the above techniques work, so choose the one you enjoy the most or that works best for you.

Quick relaxation: facial massage
Sit quietly, close your eyes and relax. Then using your middle and index fingers, slowly and gently rub small circles on the spot between your eyes in the centre of your forehead for a while; then move to the temples at both sides of your forehead and massage them together. Keep it up for a minute or two then sit quietly and enjoy the feeling. Or maybe you can persuade a friend to do it for you, which feels even better.

Joining a club – an alternative to relaxation or meditation
If you still feel ultra nervous before public speaking, you might consider joining a group which puts you in the public eye and lets you develop both confidence and skills. The university drama club is good for this, and as a bonus it usually has great parties that are full of interesting people! More formal are groups like Toastmasters, which train you in public speaking and give you practice. It is a strain at first if you are shy, but it gets easier and you will learn valuable skills that will last for life.

SHOWTIME! DELIVERING THAT PAPER

Of the three elements of an oral paper (content, organisation and presentation) you have already done the first two and only the presentation is left. How do you set about it?

Get there early!
It will increase your tension if you are running late so try to get there in good time. Organise any materials you brought with you neatly. It is uncommon to use OHTs in orals but if you are going to use any, check they are still in the order you want to use them (you remembered to number them didn't you? See Chapter 10, page 148). When people are seated and the hour arrives, pass round your handout if you have one. If you are facing a large group, it is quicker to split the pile into two or more and send them in different directions.

Time to talk basic body language
You need to sit up straight, shoulders back, head up, with poise. It's surprising how many people's opinions of your presentation can be affected by your posture.

Start by quickly looking round the group
Try to look briefly in everybody's eyes as you do this, then introduce the topic by reading out the title: "Today I am going to examine..."

Moving from one section to another
It is good to give signposts for the listeners, so that they know where you and they are as you move to a new section. You can do this by numbers, e.g. "The second cause", "The third

cause", etc., or you can state the name of the section firmly, e.g. "Turning to the results of the action..." It also helps if you pause slightly before you switch sections. If you glance up as you do this and get some eye contact, it pushes your presentation along nicely.

Ignore the late-comers
There are usually a few students who wander in after the start. Ignore them completely unless they apologise to you, in which case smile and nod but do not speak to these unspeakables! You should never stop to give them a handout or explain what they have missed for two reasons: first, this would break your flow, and second, it penalises and will probably irritate many of those who bothered to come on time. If you left a pile of handouts on the table, somebody else might slide one over to the poor time-keepers, but don't you worry about it.

Running over time
If you are running late, the staff member may intervene and ask you to finish quickly. If this happens to you, smile politely and say "Three minutes?" or longer if you think you can get away with it. When the guy in charge agrees (they almost always do!), look at your watch, and make sure you keep to that limit. You can simply read out the headings you would have liked to cover, point out you would be happy to answer questions about those bits (a sneaky and often effective way of getting the information in later!), and then jump straight to your conclusion which you can read in full. Don't forget you can remind people about the handout if you used one, and where you would have gone if you had the time.

LEARNING TO SPEAK BODY LANGUAGE

Poor body language can earn you lower marks if the assessor is unimpressed. This is particularly the case in role-playing sessions. It may sound a bit unfair but life's like that.

Look out for any nervous habits of yours
When anxious, people tend to do unattractive things, like:
- Twisting their fingers and wringing their hands.
- Desperately seeking security by clutching their jacket or dress.

- Coiling or pulling at their hair – or chewing the ends of long strands.
- Fiddling with pens, buttons, ties or skirts.
- Touching and pulling at their ears, beards or eyebrows.
- Scratching themselves.
- Biting their nails and picking at or gnawing hangnails.

Check yourself as you speak, or ask a close friend to observe you and report back. If you have any such bad habits, work at eliminating them. Such movements distract the listeners and reduce the impact of what you have to say. A good rule is to keep your hands away from your face and head at all times. Watch how TV news presenters do it – they are professionals!

Using your voice well
Listen to the sound of your own voice as you read aloud. If your voice is naturally high-pitched or shrill, try to lower it consciously while delivering the paper. Listeners tend to take deeper voices more seriously, which is a real shame if you normally sound like Minnie Mouse. People can often lower the pitch of their voice over time by humming a few long low notes each day for a minute or two (it's rumoured that Prime Minister Margaret Thatcher did that and her voice really did seem to deepen as her career progressed). Stop at once if it hurts at all: you don't wish to damage your vocal chords.

In your choice of language, you should avoid all slang, swearwords or street jargon unless you deliberately use it on rare occasions for special effect.

☺ Be careful when in a supermarket not to talk loudly about the far queue. ☺

Read it like you believe it
Do your best to keep it interesting! Frank Sinatra and Billie Holiday both used to sing the words of songs as if they really meant them. When you are speaking, try to do the same! Put stress where it helps, e.g. "Now the exciting thing is…." needs to have emphasis on "exciting". Modulate your voice: make it loud when you want to emphasise something, and softer (but audible) when it is less important. It's a good idea to pause a bit and look round before you make a vital statement – that will make them pay attention! If you notice that someone is nodding off (clearly they had a

late night and it is no reflection on the quality of your presentation) you can suddenly raise your voice which normally snaps them out of it.

To summarise on voice use
It is a good idea to try to modulate your voice and keep altering it in some way when you speak. You can:
- Consciously change its depth and volume.
- Vary your delivery speed. And pause a little between sections or before an important point.
- Try to add warmth to your voice when it is appropriate.
- Keep it interesting and try not to drone on at one level.

QUESTIONS, QUESTIONS

If you get a question that you cannot answer, it's usually best to tell the truth – if you do not know, say so. However, it's a good idea to find something relevant to say immediately, e.g. "However, we might feel that looking at the temperature of the reaction that…" or "In this area, some have speculated that…" which partially retrieves the initiative. You can then glance away from the last and awkward questioner and quickly ask for another question!

If you get a really difficult question you can buy time and make the questioner feel good with stalling phrases like: "I'm glad you asked that"; "That's a very good question"; "That really is an interesting point"; or "That puts us into a fascinating area…" However, if a questioner offers an example or analogy that contradicts what you have said, you must immediately refuse to accept that analogy or you can be guaranteed to end up in deep trouble.

CASE STUDIES

Aziz enjoys his first presentation
With his maturity and growing experience in amateur dramatics, Aziz looks forward to the challenge and does well. He prepares a neat and helpful handout, talks well, uses lots of eye contact and is most persuasive. He receives a mark of A- and is pleased with this.

Betty finds her oral a trial
Betty was unable to sleep the night before and is a bundle of nerves on the day. She prepares an excellent paper but her presentation is unimpressive. She is nervous and it shows. She speaks rapidly and has to be asked to slow down two or three times. She also twists her hair in the fingers of one hand as she reads aloud in a timid voice. However, her handout is good and the content of the paper is even better. The tutor is sharp enough to recognise the merit of the content but is unduly influenced by her manner and she only gets a mark of B, which disappoints her as she feels she had dealt with the question very well, which in fact she had.

Charlie takes it lightly
Charlie did not want to present his paper and feels rather scared though he hides it well. The paper is rather lightweight, his presentation somewhat boring, and he tends to drone on. He is lucky to scrape a pass mark from a tutor who happens to feel merciful that day. The tutor holds him back after the class and suggests that a bit more work is needed all round, and temporarily baffles poor Charlie by telling him that he needs to use more elbow grease. The tutor also points out that Charlie is letting himself down and he really could do better if he would just try a little harder. It certainly gives Charlie something to think about, but will he respond to the good advice?

DISCUSSION POINTS

1. Do you have any nervous habits? (If you don't know, ask your friends to tell you honestly.) Have you noticed if they have any? Why not ask if they'd like you to help identify any of their weaknesses in return?

2. Do you naturally speak quickly or slowly? Do you have a light or deep voice? Do you keep saying "Er", "Urm", "Yeah?" or something similar when talking? What can you do to improve your speaking and get rid of such bad habits?

3. What ways of combatting stress do you know about? Have you tried any? How well did it work for you? Do you practise relaxing every day?

SUMMARY

- It's best to write out your oral and read it aloud, especially in your first-year.
- Try to guess what questions you might be asked in your tutorial and think up possible replies that you can make.
- Consider preparing a handout when you are giving a tutorial; if you do this, make sure you have enough copies for each person.
- Do a dry run first.
- Practise a relaxation technique regularly; doing it each day is best.
- Make regular eye contact with the audience.
- Slow your speech down and do not gabble.
- Guard against fidgeting and other nervous habits.
- Listen to yourself speaking and use your voice to good effect.

7. Write on baby! Way to go!

If your school used to let you have several bites at the cherry
Some schools allow students first to go and talk to a teacher about what to put in an essay; then to hand in a draft essay and get comments back; and finally to submit the essay proper. At university you are expected simply to prepare, write, and put the essay in – and that's it.

Preparing to write
Writing up is simply the last stage of the assignment process. Always be sure you know what you think and wish to say before you start to write. "I cannot write" often really means "I have not read and thought enough and do not know what I really want to say". It's common to prepare several different outlines before you are ready to write.

It's time to do the essay
You must write out your essay properly in sentences and never do it in note form. Write it on a computer if you can; it is easy to move sections around, spell-check it, and print it up. At the printing stage, it is a good idea to set wide margins on both sides of the paper as this encourages the marker to make more comments and these are valuable.

If you have any diagrams to put in, it is usually acceptable to draw these neatly using a ruler and pen. There are excellent drawing programs for computers (CAD – computer assisted design) but they take quite some time to get to grips with.

If you do not have access to a computer (rare), then typing up your essay is the next best way. Try not to put in a handwritten assignment, which looks poor, and can earn you lower marks if the assessor gets fed up trying to read it. If you must write by hand, use black or dark blue ink, and remember to leave wide margins to encourage comments. However you write it, you should draw any diagrams and figures carefully using a ruler, and if they are complex use more than one colour. It's best not to pick red, because the marker may wish to use red to correct or add to the diagram and you never want to annoy a marker.

ESSAY TIPS – A LIST OF THINGS TO AVOID

"Before I answer this question I shall..."
Never begin with this phrase; it ensures you are sidetracked at once; it automatically causes you to answer a question that you were not asked; and it is likely to convince the marker that you are not all that bright. Disasterville!

Lyk, dude, it's so-o-o kwl n gr8 yeah? – any 1 no y? Ezpz m8! Geddit?
Right! Now I have your attention, texting-spelling, gangsta rap, slang and colloquialisms have no place in written essays. Note, however, that in oral presentations a judicious use of slang or the vernacular can sometimes be effective as long as it is in very small doses.

Humour
Few people have the gift of being able to write amusingly and their efforts to entertain are sometimes painful to read. Unless you've ever been asked who writes your material or else your name is Woody Allen or Stephen Fry you'd better avoid trying to be funny.

> ☺ Sign in an English butcher's shop: "Buy our sausages – you'll never get better." ☺

Abbreviations in essays – take care!
You must avoid all short forms like "can't", "won't" and "isn't" and write the words out in full. Written English is a bit different from spoken English. (I deliberately broke several rules in this book in order to make it more accessible – don't do as I do, do as I say!)

You should be aware that the first time you use an acronym you should spell it out, for example "The Organisation of Petroleum Exporting Countries (OPEC)..."; after that you can use the acronym alone without further explanation.

Using brackets
These (when used often) tend to give (at least to some people) a feeling of choppiness (or breathlessness) and slow down the communication of ideas (or anything else) and suggest (to the critical) that you have (probably) not thought through the issue. As you can see, it's best just to avoid it.

Using oxymorons (if you're a pedant peasant it should really be oxymora)
These are phrases that contradict themselves in some way, like "pretty ugly", "original copy" or "small crowd" (and some might think "military intelligence" or "business ethics"). While not exactly wrong, they can annoy fussy people and one of these might be marking your essay. Think carefully about the words you use.

The shotgun technique
This consists of throwing in everything you know about the issue, in the hope that a few pellets will strike home, rather than answering the question. In this case it is untrue that nothing succeeds like excess. To combat it you can practise making outline answers; spend longer on organising your approach; stick to your prepared outline; keep reading the question as you write; and sprinkle a few words from it in your answer now and then.

Getting side-tracked
This means moving away from the central question asked and delving into interesting but scarcely relevant areas. An assessor is likely to conclude that you possess a scatty mind and have a less than fully logical approach. Hello bad mark! Use the same solution as for the shotgun technique.

Trying to impress by deliberate complexity
Technical jargon is usually essential at university and makes for precision in communication. Your analysis may well be complex but the expression of it should be simple. You should not deliberately set out to write long, complex sentences or use less obvious words on the grounds that you feel this is suitable for university-level work. Too often arcane words are used in invidious fashion, possibly erroneously, your meaning becomes blurred, and you can easily forestall the attainment of the exalted mark you so richly deserve; so it is judicious to eschew the non-obligatory mode of adopting obscure vocabulary in an ineffectual endeavour to obfuscate or inveigle someone into perceiving that you are a luminary. Get the message?

Producing lightweight work
Skimpy, lightweight work is easy to recognise and it lacks thorough research and preparation. Sometimes it is the result of the assignment being rushed at the last minute. If this is a problem of yours, you can start preparing earlier; search longer for information and read more; discuss it with your study-buddy or group; and spend more time thinking and planning.

Unbalanced answers
This is where, for example, you have covered the cases for and against some proposition as you were asked, but you argued the case *for* in six lines then spent the next six pages arguing against it. To tackle this you can compare the number of points in your outline answer and the amount written for each section then try to make these a bit more equal (exact equality is not needed).

Badly organised work
Badly organised work may have been researched nicely but the information hasn't been put together properly and therefore the question won't have been answered well. To counter this you could practise making outline answers regularly; try to make several different ones for the same question; or practise competitive outline answers with your study-buddy or group.

Careless work
This includes things like misspellings, ungrammatical English, use of incorrect words (like "their" instead of "there" or that awful "of" instead of "have"), and repetitions. To tighten up your work, use the spell checker on your computer and try its grammar checker (although they are still pretty primitive). Before handing in your essay it is a good idea to wait a day before reading it again for the final polishing and improving. The eye tends to read in what it expects to see, and a piece that seemed perfect yesterday can often be improved and gain you extra marks. And of course you should generally try harder and take more care.

Personal answers
There is room for your personal opinion, but avoid scattering "I" throughout the essay. If you tend to do this, you might go through

searching for "I"s when finished and get rid of most of them. You could choose to restrict "I" to the conclusion. Note that phrases such as "Some suggest..." or "It has been pointed out that..." can often replace an "I".

Using "ought", "should" and "must"
At university you are expected to be logical, analytical, creative and scientific. Words like "ought" are too personal and prescriptive. Best avoid them! Rephrasing is necessary along the lines of "In order to achieve X (the government could ...)"; or "Of the above choices, many might prefer..."

☺   Dyslexics of the world: untie.   ☺

Sexist language
Avoid using "he" when referring to a professional person or role model as it could well be a "she". Figure 6 provides a short list of words to avoid and their preferred alternatives – remember that you do not wish to alienate the person marking your work. Also ask your university women's group if they have a list they can let you have – go on! If you're a man they are likely to be well pleased, once they get over the shock. You can use "s/he" but it does look rather clumsy to some, especially if it has to be followed later by "him/her". A neat trick is to put the word into the plural – "Doctors" then becomes "they" later, which avoids the problem.

Figure 6. Some preferred non-sexist words

Not liked	Preferred
Actress	Actor
Authoress	Author
Chairman	Chair or Chairperson
Gentleman's agreement	Hand-shake agreement
Man and wife	Partners, or husband and wife
Man-hours	Work-time or person-hours
Man-made	Artificial or synthetic
Workman	Worker

Personifying countries and institutions
You are better off not saying "she" for France or "they" for an organisation; these are *things* and really call for an "it" (we make an

exception for ships). Watch out for singular and plural problems also: an institution or a committee is not a "they" but an "it".

Using extreme language
If you keep saying "extremely", "tremendously", "enormously" or "remarkably" you are probably overstating your case. If you use any of the following you are definitely doing so: alarmingly, amazingly, catastrophic, disastrous, fantastic, grotesquely, huge, meteoric, stupendous, tremendous, unprecedented, or wonderful.

For those suffering from this hideous malady (OK, I plead guilty at this particular point) you can think about what you really believe and choose your words more carefully; use a thesaurus for a weaker alternative; and, finally, read over at the end and knock out any extreme words you find. Sometimes you can replace them with a weaker word, but often they can simply disappear completely.

☺   I've told you a million times not to exaggerate.   ☺

Reaching conclusions without good evidence
Believing something to be true is not evidence, nor is the fact that one book said it – another book may say exactly the reverse. If not tested by data, a theory or model remains no more than an opinion. Be sure you provide enough data to back up your conclusions.

Keep an eye open for spurious correlations or any hidden third causes – if statistics suggest that changes in the number of children born in Sweden vary with the number of storks breeding on one lake (as we are told they do), we cannot assume that storks bring babies!

Labelling people or ideas for a cheap shot
It is fairly easy to hang a label around the neck of someone of whom we disapprove and tarnish them with a poor image. "Fascist" is regularly and incorrectly used as a critical description in this way, as was "communist" in the United States, especially during the McCarthy era in the 1950s. Equally, the "straw person" approach is suspect: this is where we start by defending someone but in a deliberately weak way, then we proceed to knock down the defence with gusto. This can be fun, but does not produce balanced, quality work. Try to be more even-handed.

Political or cultural bias
This is hard to spot in one's own writing, but perhaps easier in the statements of others. Common forms of bias are political, racial, social,

and religious. Watch for it carefully in your own work as well as that of others. You can also ask your study-buddy if he or she notices anything like this about you.

Rambling answers
If you cannot keep to set-length guidelines or your essays seem to be much longer than other peoples' you are probably rambling. Markers' comments might indicate it also. In an effort to tighten up you can take more care with your outlines; prune your text heavily; never repeat statements you have already made; and avoid "as I said before..." which automatically means a repetition.

ESSAY TIPS – WATCH FOR THESE WHEN WRITING ESSAYS

When a question includes a quotation – beware!
As soon as you spot a quotation, alarm bells should ring. It often indicates something tricky, for example the quote may be only partially true, true only under certain circumstances, or barely true at all. That quotation frequently means you need to adopt a somewhat critical approach.

Keeping measurements consistent
Stick either to metric or imperial measures. For example, do not use feet and inches in one part of your paper and then metres and millimetres in another. Similarly, do not mix fractions and percentages when making comparisons. You might notice that some journalists are guilty of this but we should make allowances for the poor creatures.

Plural and singular
If your subject is plural the verb form must also be plural, however much the two may be separated in a long sentence: "the country...are" is just plain wrong. To avoid this, read over carefully at the end.

Adding a bibliography
You may be asked for a bibliography, but if not consider putting one in anyway. It tends to impress the marker and shows you are trying hard.

Should you photocopy your assignment?
If you wrote it by hand or typed it, make sure you photocopy it before handing it in. Essays do get lost (when I was a student two of mine did!) and it is a major hassle having to rewrite the whole thing or try to persuade

the university you did put it in. A photocopy brings peace of mind. If you wrote it on a computer as advised you need not bother to copy it as you have it on file and should have made a back-up which you keep well away from the computer.

TRIED THE ABOVE AND I STILL HAVE PROBLEMS WRITING

You can ask if your university provides assistance
Some universities have an essay adviser, or similar, whose job it is to assist those who have trouble writing. If your university provides this service, make an appointment, take a marked essay or two along to show, and then discuss your problems. There are also books available to help with essay writing. Try for instance *Your Own Words* by Judith Wainwright and Jackie Hutton (Nelson, 1992) which some students have found helpful.

YOU TOO CAN BE STYLISH

Improving your writing style is not easy to do, nor will it happen quickly, but for long-term gains you can:

1. Practise writing a little each day
Like most things, good writing comes with practice, it does not just happen. Choose some topic in your area of interest, plan an answer then write about it for perhaps fifteen minutes. Select each word with care and try to make your choice of words reflect exactly what you think and feel. Aim for an economy of words and simplicity of expression. Use as few adjectives and adverbs as possible, and make the nouns and verbs do all the work. If the topic is relevant to your university work, keep the piece of paper on file as it could prove useful later.

Make sure you are writing sentences (mostly they have a noun, a verb and an object – seek out a basic English grammar book if you have trouble here. Some find useful Raymond Murphy *et al*, *English Grammar In Use with Answers and CD ROM: A Self-study Reference and Practice Book for Elementary Students of English;* Cambridge UP; there is also Volume Two for Intermediate level students; both are often available on eBay).

2. Avoid using the same word in close proximity
It is not good to use a word twice in the same sentence or nearby, for example in the same or even the next few paragraphs. If you can't think of a substitute, look in a thesaurus for one. Some computer word processors have one built in and you can use an online site such as synonym.com (see Appendix A).

3. Read more
Reading poetry and good novels steeps you in stylish writing and word-use, which might help you to improve. How do you find good novels? Each year there are annual nominations of books for the Man Booker prize and these are considered to be well-written; other sources include the Costa Book awards and the Orange prize. You can also ask in your Humanities or English department for suggestions on some good novels to read, and you might tell them why you want the information. With a poem you should read it several times looking for the main meaning and any hidden ones. In both novels and poems, you can examine each word and its relationship to the words around. The adjectives and adverbs used often merit attention. As an exercise, you can consider why a particular word was chosen – and see if you can find one you like better. It's not easy to succeed here but trying it regularly can improve your writing a lot. You are concentrating on word choice and widening your mind.

> ☺ Some students would rather get bad marks than think – in fact they do. Try not to be one of them! ☺

Got my essay back: what does my mark mean?
Figure 7 shows you a typical marking scenario. Individual institutions vary however; for instance, not all will have a grade of "pass conceded" and the percentages for different grades may well be different from those shown here. You should ask about the system and its actual meaning at your own university.

A LATE ASSIGNMENT IS AN UNHAPPY ASSIGNMENT

You may lose marks if you put an assignment in late, and eventually it will not be accepted for marking at all. Worse, once you put in one late assignment, you tend to fall behind with the next. It is then hard to catch up so that a depressing chain begins. There go the dominoes! In your rush to finish, do not forget to put your name and subject on the assignment, and anything else required like the course code or marker's name.

Figure 7. Typical marking systems with approximate equivalents

GRADE	MEANING	GRADE	PERCENT
HD	High Distinction	A++	Approx. 85%+
D	Distinction	A- to A+	Approx. 75–84%
C	Credit	B- to B++	Approx. 65–74%
P	Pass	C- to C++	Approx. 50–64%
PC	Pass Conceded	D++	Approx. 47–49%
F	Fail	D	Under 47%

Being late could be the death of me. Why did it happen?

If bad time management was responsible
Make a new and improved weekly timetable. You can also flag assignments earlier in your diary. Think positive! You are learning the valuable skill of time management that you obviously need and you will possess for all your working life.

If putting off starting to prepare your assignment was responsible
You might have been afraid of the assignment. Never let fear crush you and stop you beginning. Take a look at "I've really got to start that assignment", page 77.

What to do if you are running late
You can try asking for an extension but make sure you have an acceptable reason ready. Not being organised is not good enough, but sickness usually is and family problems might be. Ask early enough so that if your request is refused you can submit something, however quickly and badly

written. That will get you some marks at least, whereas no submission gains you no marks.

IF THE WORST HAPPENS AND YOU FAIL AN ASSIGNMENT

If you are unlucky enough to fail an assignment, study Figure 8 to help you assess where you went wrong and what you can do to try to remedy it next time. This would be a good time to rethink things and try to improve, for you do not wish to end up on the rubbish tip at the end of the universe.

You can of course try appealing the grade, which might get you a pass. However, if you do this more than once, it is likely to go on your record and that will not help you to get a good reference from a staff member when you are later looking for a job.

CASE STUDIES

Aziz is disappointed with his mark

Aziz wants a high mark. After an earlier shaky start, he now does adequate preparation but when writing if a new idea pops into his mind he immediately builds it in, temporarily ignoring his planned outline. Finally he returns to his plan, causing the essay to lose some of its logical structure. He types properly using all his fingers but does it at high speed and leaves a few uncorrected spelling errors. He receives a mark of C+ and is disappointed. He promises himself next time he will stick with the planned outline and work to avoid careless mistakes. Maybe it's time to buy a personal computer, and he knows of a good second-hand one. It is not the latest with all the new bells and whistles but it is more than adequate for his needs. This is a sensible decision – and it's cheap!

Betty is pleased with her excellent mark

Betty also wants a top mark. She discusses the question with her study-buddy, organises several skeleton answers and digs out much information. Writing up, she sticks faithfully to her outline. She adopts a tight, analytical approach and as well as the standard textbook answer provides her own insights. She uses a computer to write, consults the built-in thesaurus (not great but adequate), spell-checks at the end, then prints up. She receives a mark of A++. Naturally, she is over the moon!

Charlie's mark reflects the effort he put in

Charlie only wants passing grades as his aim is just to scrape a degree while having a good time. He left it to the last minute to begin the essay, read his lecture notes, then wrote the answer from his head without any planning. His grade was a fail but despite his lack of effort it was only just a fail. His department decided to award him a "pass conceded" with the aim of admonishing him but at the same time offering encouragement to do a little bit better. The borderline fail shook him a bit and he feels determined to work harder, start earlier, and prepare better next time. It won't be easy as he has some catching up to do and, even more difficult, he has to unlearn bad habits – but at least he wants to improve.

DISCUSSION POINTS

1. What sort of writing or preparation habits do you have that could reduce your marks?

2. Write down as many words as you can think of in five minutes that can have a sexist connotation. What substitute word can you think of for each?

3. Have you ever been late with a school assignment or task at work? Why was that? How did you explain being late? Can you invent three good reasons for requesting an extension now that you are at university? (Keep these – you never know!)

Figure 8. What to do if you fail an assignment

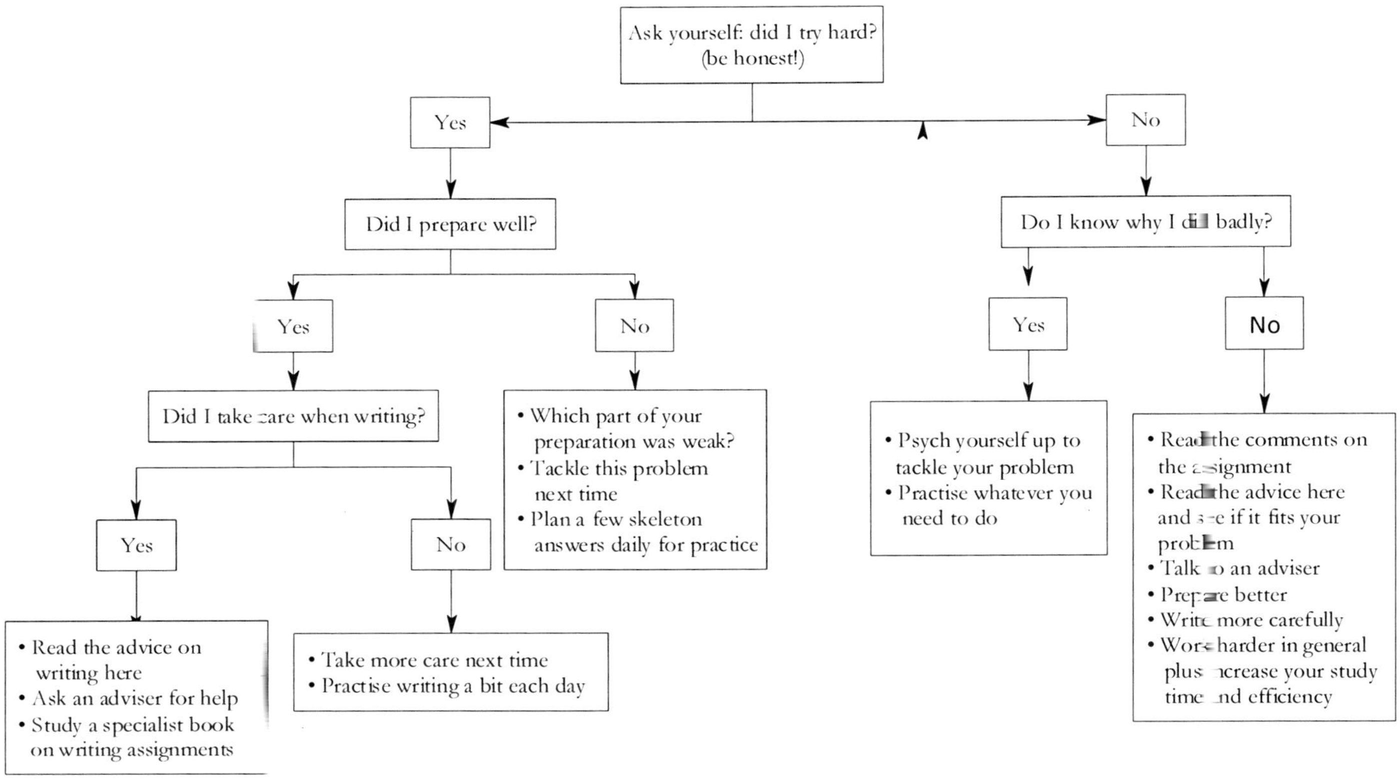

```
                    Ask yourself: did I try hard?
                           (be honest!)
                    ┌──────────┴──────────┐
                   Yes                    No
                    │                     │
              Did I prepare well?    Do I know why I did badly?
              ┌─────┴─────┐          ┌─────┴─────┐
             Yes          No        Yes          No
              │            │         │            │
   Did I take care    • Which part   • Psych    • Read the comments on
      when writing?     of your        yourself    the assignment
   ┌─────┴─────┐        preparation    up to    • Read the advice here
  Yes          No       was weak?      tackle     and see if it fits your
   │            │     • Tackle this    your       problem
   │            │       problem        problem  • Talk to an adviser
   │            │       next time    • Practise • Prepare better
   │            │     • Plan a few     whatever • Write more carefully
   │            │       skeleton       you need • Work harder in general
   │            │       answers        to do      plus increase your study
   │            │       daily for                 time and efficiency
   │            │       practice
   │            │
   │       • Take more care next time
   │       • Practise writing a bit each day
   │
 • Read the advice on writing here
 • Ask an adviser for help
 • Study a specialist book on writing assignments
```

113

SUMMARY

- It's best to write assignments on a computer and print them out; avoid presenting handwritten essays if possible.
- Always make sure you know what you think before you start to write.
- Answer the question asked and do not get side-tracked.
- Stay away from slang, colloquial English, and attempts at humour.
- Avoid abbreviations, lots of brackets, and mixing units of measurement.
- Do not strive for complex sentences or use particularly obscure words to try to impress.
- It's best to analyse, rather than describe.
- Do not simply put down all you know about the issue.
- Organise your work clearly and make sure you have a balanced answer.
- Avoid sexist language, a too personal approach, and extreme words.
- Avoid reaching conclusions without good evidence, or labelling ideas for a cheap shot.
- Keep a copy of your assignments on the computer, on a removable drive or floppy disc, or photocopy it.
- Get those assignments in on time!

8. They're going to examine me, but I feel fine

You should try to revise regularly throughout the term – ignore the smart guy who says that if it wasn't for the last minute, nothing would ever get done. Regular revision can help prevent the exam blues; I hope by now you set aside some time every day to read over a few of your notes. Half an hour is often enough, but it depends on your personality, your memory, your enthusiasm and so on. A good revision technique is to read your notes and the skeleton answers you made earlier, and also to devise new outlines to questions from old exam papers, tutorials, the textbook, or the study guide. You will probably have a short break between the end of teaching and the beginning of exams. Use this time wisely – it is your last chance for revision so you should make the most of it.

GETTING READY FOR THE EXAM

Avoiding emotional upsets
There may be fifty ways to leave your lover but this is a rotten time to choose to break off with your boyfriend or girlfriend. Wait until after the exams to end it all. Nothing should disturb your mental equilibrium, and emotional conflicts are high on the list of things that can pull down the standard of your work.

Make a new plan, man!
Try making a plan for the best use of your time. Allocate roughly equal time for each subject, but make sure you give a bit more to your weakest area. This can improve your overall performance, because it is generally easier to raise your mark from 40 to 50 per cent than from 80 to 90 per cent.

Fragment the day, Ray
Break your study day into chunks. Remember to study for your optimal length of time, whatever that is, and then take a short break between revision sessions.

Those notes must be read, Fred
For most people it is better to do this topic by topic. You could also go through your textbook and read the bits you highlighted, as well as practise drawing diagrams (if applicable to your subject).

Combat that stress, Bess
You already know various relaxation techniques and should have decided on the one you like best; it's a good idea to do it regularly (it works better with practice). Use your preferred one daily in the lead up to the exams. Be aware also that steady revision throughout the term together with a good revision programme in the two or three weeks before the exams help you to keep your stress levels under control.

No new work, Kirk
It is a waste of your precious time going to the library at this stage looking for new information or reading up new stuff. You're now in pure revision time!

You tell me yours, I'll tell you mine
It is good to work with your study-buddy or group for part of each day if possible, either discussing topics or going through questions and brainstorming answers. Such sessions help to break up the tedium of sitting reading notes all day and are an aid to memory. Play games for variety. With a topic, you might all sit and read it up from your individual notes for say five to ten minutes, then one person explains it to the others, and they then question, criticise and comment. You reinforce knowledge and might get some new and interesting insights, as you are working from different notes. Two topics and a short break often seem to work well.

You can select a question and discuss a possible answer as a group. Alternatively, each person could draft an outline answer to the same question for five minutes and you then compare them by passing these outlines around the group. A really good composite answer can often be devised from these efforts.

The night before the exam
It is best to leave the night before an examination free. The little bit you will manage to stuff in your memory can easily be smaller than the amount you inadvertently knock out. Last minute cramming often means that none shall sleep and you don't need that. It is best to relax quietly and go to bed around your usual time, or maybe just a little bit later to encourage you to drop off.

I HATE EXAMS BUT I'VE GOT TO DO THEM

Getting there must not be hard to do
A few days before the exam, check that the date, time and room you put in your diary are all correct so you do not inadvertently get there half an hour late or even on the wrong day. The night before, make sure you set your alarm so you wake up in good time and avoid hassles and worries. It's best not to try to study before you leave. Eat something and get there in good time. If you go in by bus, you might catch the one earlier than usual to be sure. If you have an ancient car that won't always start, consider getting a lift or choosing a more reliable means of transport.

When you get there, try not to stand around discussing possible questions and their answers with friends. This process, like revising the night before, can be counter-productive. It can also start you worrying which you definitely do not need. Use Figure 9 to help you check that you are prepared for the day of the exam.

Once in the exam room – don't panic!
Go into the exam room as soon as they will let you, and, if it is allowed, find a seat where you will feel comfortable; then lay out your kit and relax. If you feel nervously excited, use this emotion to your advantage. Concentrate your mind on the challenge ahead and your wish to win, whilst telling yourself you are happy to face this confrontation and overcome it. You can also use one of the quick relaxation techniques if you feel the need. When you are allowed to do so, read the instructions carefully, and do everything they tell you. Read through the questions

several times, select which ones you will tackle, and mark them with a tick or number. *Ignore all the other questions henceforth:* reading them again is a waste of time and can make you feel worried. You must attempt the required number of questions – check again to make sure you are not doing too few or too many – I've seen this happen s-o-o-o often. With a multi-part question, make sure you have answered all the parts.

Figure 9. A checklist for the day before your exam

• Am I sure that I know where the room is and what time the exam starts?
• Have I set a reliable alarm clock and also asked others to wake me in good time?
• Do I have my kit of coloured pens, pencils, eraser, ruler, correcting fluid, a calculator, some water, some sweets to suck, and a watch? If your native language is not English, a dictionary can be of help, if this is allowed.
• Is my transport reliable?
• Have I thought about how I can safely get there in time if something goes wrong? This might require a taxi fare.

Biding your time and dividing your time
It is best to divide your time up between questions and allow, say, fifteen minutes for reading over at the end. Give each question the same time unless one question is worth more marks, in which case you give it more time. Pace yourself when writing – four questions of decent length and reasonably well done usually earn more marks than three voluminous ones plus a few scrappy lines for the fourth. If you are running late, the last question can often be done in note form and this will normally get you some marks at least.

☺   Testing animals is bad – besides they always get the answers wrong.   ☺

If you fail to plan, you plan to fail
Making an outline of your intended answer is not time wasted but time invested – good answers get good marks. A good answer includes an introduction, body and conclusion. The body contains the basic points,

organised in logical fashion, and written up legibly. This will not happen by accident; if you simply seize your pen and start scribbling, you can expect to get a poor mark. Ignore the idiot next to you who does that; the guy is like a really obvious question – a no-brainer. You should read the question carefully both before and as you make the skeleton answer.

You can usually plan your answer in the back of the exam book but remember to cross it out before handing the book in. Some prefer to make their outline on the back of the question paper itself.

Do answer the question asked – an important reminder!
With this in mind, never start your answer with "Before I deal with this I shall..."; it means you are sidetracking yourself immediately. Also, resist the temptation to put down all you know about the topic – yes, it's tempting to try to impress the marker with how good you are but this shotgun technique, firing a lot of pellets and hoping that a few hit the target, ensures that you are not *answering* the question, merely talking about the issue. Your mark will suffer if you do this.

Using subheads
In many subjects, good use of subheads, carefully underlined with a ruler (but not in red remember), helps you gain marks. However, a few courses like English literature and foreign languages may not allow them. Subheads make your outline clear so that the assessor can rapidly see the logic of your approach and the extent of your knowledge. It is particularly good if your handwriting is poor, because it makes marking easier and this pleases the one and only person who decides how many marks you will get.

☺ Most medic students know that a semicolon is not really half a large ☺
intestine.

Starting your main answer
Do not waste time writing out the words of the question – just put its number in the margin. Your introduction should be short, and therefore the start of the body of your answer ought to be on the first page. Unless instructed otherwise, start a new page for each question: it's their paper,

it does not cost you anything, and the benefit is that it not only looks better but the marker can find your answers easily.

Please, lend an ear to my pleas! Do write legibly
Try your hardest to write neatly. If no one can read any of it, expect no marks. If only parts of it can be read, you will only get some of your possible marks. In addition, you've annoyed the assessor.

Let me draw you a diagram
An old cliché, often ascribed to the Chinese, has it that "one picture is worth a thousand words", and in some disciplines assessors like to see diagrams and these can get you marks. You need not waste time making your diagrams works of art – as long as your diagrams are neat (use a ruler) and correct it is enough. Depending on your subject, one diagram per question is not too much, and several more might be necessary. Make sure you label all the parts of the diagram properly.

It's best to avoid the exam post-mortem
When you have finished your paper, mutter "for this relief much thanks" and move on. It is a mistake to hang around outside the exam room discussing the questions you just answered with your fellow victims as this only helps to increase your level of stress. You need to forget the exam that you just did, and if you have to do another one on the same day you should try to relax; if the next exam is not for a few days, you can go back to preparing for it.

PUTTING YOU TO THE TEST: OTHER EXAM FORMATS

This section looks at alternative forms of testing, including:

- Multiple-choice quizzes.
- Write-in answers.
- True–false tests.

Multiple-choice quizzes are increasingly being used in tertiary level education. This is not because they are thought to be intrinsically better than essay-style exams but because they are the natural, if ugly, offspring of governments trying to get education on the cheap. Student numbers have rapidly increased but government money has not: without a proportional increase in staff, quicker forms of assessment and marking have to be used. The use of computers has speeded up multiple-choice marking considerably so in many disciplines you now need to know how to cope with multiple-choice tests and exams.

You should check recent exam papers and your course syllabus to see what type of quiz will be set and practise doing a few of them. Your textbook or study guide may have examples – and there is a chance the course convenor will choose at least some of these questions for the exam, which will give you an edge.

☺   Exams make me testy.   ☺

Improving your multiple-choice scores

Choosing the "best" answer
With all multiple-choice quizzes you select the best answer from the choices offered. This is the one that applies normally or covers the most options. See the following question:

A seagull is:
    A) A bird.
    B) A large web-footed bird.
    C) A large web-footed bird that eats fish.
    D) None of the above.

The best answer is C, even if A and B are correct, because it covers the most. There is never any point writing annotations on multiple-choice papers explaining your choice, because the computer cannot read them. Writing "Some gulls eat inland and never see a fish" in the margin and then choosing B, gets you a wrong mark.

Moving on if stuck
If you cannot answer a particular question you should go immediately to the next one and not waste time fretting over one that seems particularly difficult. There will probably be others later that you can answer. You must get through the entire paper if you are to score the highest mark you can. When you reach the end, go back to the ones that you missed earlier and start again, cycling through until either you finish or time runs out. If you do not get to the end at all, you can be sure that you are spending too long on the earlier questions and your marks will suffer. If you do not

tackle the last ten per cent of the questions, you are being marked out of 90 not 100! That way disaster lies.

Multiple-choice: in some subjects a diagram might help
It may help you to understand a question if you draw a diagram to work out what is happening. The back of the question paper and the inside back cover of the exam paper are good places, but cross the diagram out before handing your written paper in.

Take special care with tricky questions
Negative questions ("Which of the following is not a cause...") can be tricky. You might find it helps to remove the negative, ask yourself which ones *can* be a cause and cross them off, which leaves the correct answer exposed.

Dealing with the "All of the above" and "None of the above": if you decide that one offered choice cannot be true, you know "All the above" must be wrong and thus can be eliminated. If two choices contradict or are mutually incompatible, again it cannot be correct. With "None of the above", if you can determine that a single choice works then you can eliminate the "None" answer.

Always guess rather than leave blanks
Most universities give a mark for a correct answer but do not subtract a mark for a wrong one (it's easier for the machine to mark in this way). Check first to see if your university is like this: if so, it means you maximise your score by guessing those you cannot work out. If you guess, you might be right; if you fail to answer, you must be wrong. To improve the odds, before you adopt the Eeny-Meeny-Miny-Moe principle, see if you can eliminate one or two of the choices and choose between those left.

Scraping the barrel for clues
When stuck on a question, it is sometimes worth checking the lengths of the choices offered. Sometimes (but definitely not always) the correct answer is indicated by the longest choice offered. This happens if the person setting the question hedged the correct answer round with clauses to ensure it would be correct under all circumstances.

You can sometimes work out the correct multiple-choice answer by looking at the essay questions, the write-in questions or even other multiple-choice questions on the paper, as these might offer clues. Because this takes time, it is only worth doing if you have gone all the way through the questions and have started to recycle.

Improving your score for write-in answers

Choosing the right words
There may be several, probably lots, of different phrases and words that will fit the gaps. For instance "When the level of ... increases we expect to see a ... in national income or an increase in ...". In an economics exam the words "demand", "rise" and "inflation" seem required but in a geography one "floodwater", "change" and "water-born diseases" would fit. Do not panic but choose sensible words that suit the course you are doing.

How to score well on creative write-in questions
These are more common in job applications than in course assessment but some of you might face such a test. With questions like "Write down as many uses of a pencil as you can think of", you are expected to demonstrate creativity, lateral thinking, and inventiveness. You should aim to think of really original things in addition to the obvious ones. Everyone will say "writing letters" but you could add uses like "constructing a see-saw for tame mice", "using it to cast the shadow in a sun dial", or "giving it to a garden gnome to add a professional air" and similar creative and off-beat uses. You should not worry about being silly or looking foolish, because suggesting amusing uses actually tends to gain you marks. Write down as many as you can in the time allowed – to work out your mark, some assessors simply count up the number of uses you supply. If the write-in is part of a more general exam and you have time left over after reading and correcting your English, go back to this section and keep inventing new uses.

Improving your score in true–false tests

Assume the most common situation exists
Never get too clever and think the statement is usually true but under a special set of circumstances it would be false and select that one. The most obvious answer is usually the correct one in true–false tests. The really tricky questions tend to be asked in the essay section.

Look for words like "often", "frequently" and "generally"
These might well indicate it is a "true" statement as these modifying words weaken the suggestion and make it more modest by allowing for exceptions.

Similarly with words like "always", "must" or "never"
These suggest it could be a "false" statement, as only one piece of evidence to the contrary is needed to render it untrue. Note that if any one part of a long sentence is false the statement as a whole must be false.

Avoid trying to balance your true and false answers
The setters do not have a fifty per cent rule, so there is never any point in adjusting your answers to get an equal number of "yes" and "no" ones. Multiple-choice answers are similarly random and do not have one quarter allocated to each "A", "B", "C", and "D" answer.

CHEATING MAY LOOK ENTICING BUT IT IS A POOR IDEA

It may be tempting to try to smuggle notes or bits of information into the exam room on your ruler, in a pencil case, or programmed into a calculator or mobile phone, but do not bother. Rarely does your mark rely on you knowing a few facts, dates, symbols etc. The mark you get tends to reflect the overall quality of your answer, judged by things like the standard of your arguments, the logical way you tackle the question, and the weight of the evidence you marshal. The rewards for successful cheating are often surprisingly small. A good outline and argument beat a few correct facts any day. The risks of cheating are great and you might be given zero for the exam. Should you succeed in cheating, you still do not know how well you are really doing.

With course work and essay assignments it is particularly tempting to download essays from the Internet, especially if you are running short on time. It's still a bad idea though!

The downside includes:
- You have to pay for the stuff.
- You learn nothing about the subject matter.
- You fail to develop the skills you will need in life.
- You are unlikely to remember much about the content later.
- You will suffer in the exam room if that topic comes up.

- You should not train yourself to climb the ladder of success wrong by wrong. Bad attitudes tend to become ingrained.

CASE STUDIES

Steady revision pays off now for Aziz
Aziz is scared facing his first exam after being away from study for over a decade, but knows he has revised consistently so he hopes that he will be all right. He has a spare pen but no correcting fluid and his corrected paper looks messy with many crossings out. His natural enthusiasm takes over and he does not spend enough time selecting the questions carefully. He plans his answers but not as well as he might. He gets a B+ but had hoped for an A.

To Betty it is an exciting challenge
She looks forward to the exam but keeps this fact quiet as she rightly suspects that this view will not make her popular and she needs to hang on to the relatively few friends she has made. She knows she will do well and has revised steadily over the whole term. She takes a full kit in, chooses the questions carefully and plans them out. She gets an A+ and is very happy indeed; but it's a shame she has no one special to share her joy with.

But fear is the key for Charlie
Charlie panicked before the exam when he realised he had done no preparation. He revised like mad for three days, staying up late at night to do so, and is really tired on the day. He has no kit and does not plan his answers before writing. His pen runs out and he has to finish in pencil. He fails, but not badly enough to get him thrown out – this time at least.

DISCUSSION POINTS

1. If you have seven days in which to revise and four subjects, how would you organise your revision schedule? Why in that particular way?

2. What might you do if you get to the exam room far too early? What would not be a good idea?

3. In the exam room, once you have selected the particular questions that you will tackle, would you prefer to plan them all out immediately or do them on the basis of plan-one-write-one?

SUMMARY

- Most of your revision should be done steadily throughout the term.
- Make a plan for the best use of the time available for your final revision.
- In this revision period you should refuse to do any new work.
- It helps to vary your activity when revising.
- Working with your study-buddy or group makes a good and useful change.
- Get to the exam room early, take a kit, and settle down in a comfortable place if possible.
- Allocate your time for each question carefully.
- Always plan out your answer before you start to write.
- Answer the question asked.
- Use subheads if it is allowed – it usually is.
- Write legibly, do not use red or pencil, but do use diagrams if appropriate to your subject.
- With multiple-choice quizzes do not get hung up on one question; move on.
- Take special care with negative multiple-choice questions.
- Unless wrong answers are penalised, guess rather than leave a blank, but first eliminate what options you can.
- When stuck, move on quickly.
- With write-in answers, it often helps to read all the questions before filling in the answers.
- Be creative with open-ended invention questions.
- With true–false questions, look for suggestive words like "must" or "sometimes"; draw yourself a diagram if it helps you and they are common in your subject.
- Do not try to cheat! The downside of being found out is a lot bigger than the upside of a minor improvement in your work – which is only a possibility anyway.

9. Developing team skills – the passport to a better job

☺ " We must indeed all hang together, or, most assuredly, we shall all hang separately." (Benjamin Franklin, 4 July 1776) ☺

Up team, up team, up team!
In order to land a good job you need to stand out from the pack and offer something special that the employer wants. What are they looking for?

Some of the skills increasingly sought in business include the ability to:
- Work successfully in teams.
- Communicate well.
- Solve problems.
- Organise tasks in order of priority.
- Manage your time properly.
- Exercise leadership.
- Take initiatives.

Such skills on your CV can help you find a good and well-paid job more quickly – in the competition of the workplace you have to show you are as talented as Mr Ripley. In large companies, it is common to work as a group on a particular project and when it is over the team disbands. When something else needs doing, a different team will be assembled. You need to be able to do this. Apart from that special need, the days of a job for life have virtually disappeared, and many people now work for some time on contract before moving on to a new contract with a different company, possibly in another country. You need portable skills like those above to keep on getting new contracts and to cope with the rapidly changing times in which we live.

Working in a team
Some university courses require you to undertake a group project, while others offer you the chance if you want it. If you have the opportunity – take it! Ignore those who might say things like it's not a proper course, or that the lunatics are running the asylum; practice in team skills is very valuable. If you are committed to studying a particular discipline but it has no team projects, it is worth seeing if you can take such a course from another field or department which encourages this valuable kind of work.

> ☺ For the cynics amongst us, team work means never having to take all ☺
> the blame yourself.

No man is an island. Working in a team you will start to develop the above skills and others of value

- Understanding group dynamics.
- Working in cooperation with others, even people you do not naturally get along with.
- Delegating responsibility.
- Smoothing ruffled feathers.
- Building in safety margins for deadlines.
- Editing the work of others.
- Combining individual documents into one report.

WE'RE OFF! STARTING THE PROJECT

There will probably be a meeting with a staff member present who might tell you what to do in order to get the group project off the ground. Alternatively, he or she might adopt a simple "resources" role, and be available so that you can ask questions and get help when you feel you want it. In this case, they might only volunteer information if it seems to them you desperately need it.

Choosing the right leader
A mature experienced student is often the best but a good 19 year old is generally better than a hopeless 30 year old. The entire group can sit and talk about who might make a good leader but in the end you may have to take a volunteer. If the project is going to be done by an existing study-group, you will already know each other's strengths which will enable you to choose a good person. The leader's job is to organise and control without offending people, smooth over disputes that might arise, maybe liaise with the staff member, and be able to write reasonably well. Not everybody is leadership material!

You need a timetable

☺   Timetable = using a stopwatch to see how fast your furniture moves.   ☺

You should make a rough timetable so that everyone knows when things are due. The following stages are typical:
- Stage One: a brainstorming session to decide how to tackle the question. This should be finished in one meeting. If not, you will just have to get together again. If things go incredibly smoothly you could also select the members of the small teams.
- Stage Two: dividing everyone into small teams (if not done already), each of which goes off to research a part of the outline agreed in Stage One. Each small team then puts together a report which goes up to the main group.
- Stage Three: writing the draft (main) report.
- Stage Four: examining the draft report, deciding on changes, and writing the final report.
- Stage Five: may include presenting the final report in a full session before submitting it in writing to be marked.

It is desirable to incorporate a few safety margins on dates, so that if anyone is late (and somebody always will be!) it does not delay the final report.

STAGE ONE: BRAINSTORMING THE PROJECT

Unless the staff member suggests something different, as a start you might try a brainstorming session where you throw ideas around and consider the main points that might be addressed. It often helps to consider if there are different ways that the question could be tackled. A workable approach is to divide up into small groups of maybe three to six students, depending on the size of the whole group, and discuss the question for, say, ten minutes. After that, one member from each group stands up and reports what that group talked about and concluded. You can expect to get several decent and different proposals in this way. If one person writes the suggestions and ideas on the board as each short report is made, you end up with lots of varied points. After discussion, you should be able to mix and match these to get to a great final version.

STAGE TWO: WORKING IN SMALL GROUPS

Dividing up the task into parts
Once you have the broad approach agreed (Stage One) and have broken down the question into its main sections, you divide everyone into teams. Each team might work solely on one main part of the outline and a team might consist of between two and eight students, again depending on how many of you there are in all. If some parts seem likely to be more difficult you could make that team larger. Often teams emerge naturally, as friends or study-buddies like to work together.

Each team needs a leader
Someone should be in charge, to deal with issues like when and where the members will next meet, and who might go with whom to search for what. The team leader will liaise with other teams, generally pull things

together, and make sure the team report gets finished on time. It is a help if everyone knows who is in charge of the other teams as this is the contact person – a piece of paper with the contact names, telephone numbers and email addresses, as well as the section of the project they are covering, can be circulated to all. You can never tell who might want to talk to another small group, but someone probably will. In addition, you might get a useful telephone number or two.

The teams meet separately. At the first meeting you could decide whether you will work in ones or twos and what each member is going to investigate. You will need to set a date for a get-together to report progress, where any issues or problems being experienced can be discussed. In addition, you need to fix a date for the final meeting where the individual bits of information are put in and cobbled together into a team report. Don't forget to build in a safety margin of a few days before you must hand over your team report to the larger group.

Liaising with other teams
Your team might need to talk to some of the other teams to ensure that you are roughly agreeing on direction and beliefs. It might be embarrassing if four teams decide the project is good and yours believes it is bad, or your report clashes in other important ways with some of the others. It is not always essential to liaise, and to some extent it depends on the topic and the individuals involved. Just remember not to lose that list of contact names!

☺   Is there another word for "synonym"?   ☺

Writing the small team report
Each member of the team will probably need to draft a report on their individual findings that might conveniently be in note form. The team should meet to discuss these and iron out any obvious contradictions as well as determine the major thrust that the report will take. The team leader then takes these different notes and writes up the report. Your team members might wish to meet again to see it, or maybe could decide to put their trust in the leader. For safety, this report should be on computer disc or portable memory stick as well as in hard copy. At the top level, the different computer files can easily be copied and put together, using cutting, pasting, and editing. Saving in RTF format makes it easier for other people to read and use, especially if some have Macs and others PCs. The PDF format is best avoided as it is not easy to edit without special programs.

STAGE THREE: PUTTING IT TOGETHER AND ASSEMBLING THE GROUP REPORT

Deciding which person will do it

The draft report is usually best put together by the overall leader after consultations, perhaps with the leaders of the small teams. One person really has to write the draft but can usefully have a few friends to consult with. A committee is not very suitable for creative writing ("A camel is a horse designed by a committee") and is best used for drawing up guidelines and later suggesting amendments. Remember to allow enough time for this person to put it all together.

The mechanics of the process are often like this:

- The overall leader first reads the hard copies in order to get an idea of the overall thrust of the views. He or she also loads up the reports onto the computer.
- The overall leader might want to talk to the team leaders before going further, in order to ask questions and sort out any misunderstandings or check on any unclear bits.
- Then the leader might have a look at the original outline from the first brainstorming session and decide if that is still valid as a result of the actual findings. If so, the detailed outline of the report is already established. If not, then some minor tinkering with the earlier outline could be needed.
- The leader then sits at the computer and merges the files, editing, cutting and pasting, and rewriting as necessary, until one coherent and non-contradictory draft report emerges. This is a difficult but wonderful skill to develop while still at university – get it on your CV before you forget.
- A draft conclusion and introduction may also be prepared at this stage. Counter-intuitively, many people find it easier to write the conclusion first then do the introduction last, once they know what the results are!

STAGE FOUR: EXAMINING THE DRAFT REPORT

This draft report, along with the introduction and conclusion, can be circulated to all for their comments if there is time. Otherwise it will have to be distributed at a full meeting. If you are the overall leader, you really do need this approval by those below. Without it, someone might query or criticise your report later and they just might be experts, having been responsible for that particular part! You will probably find you need some changes, and perhaps significant compromises will be required. If the topic allows for differences of political opinion, this can be a stormy stage. When you have approval, subject to whatever changes have been suggested and agreed, the final report is just about there – incorporate the changes and you're done. Well, almost!

It may be required by the rules of the course that this report be presented and discussed at a plenary session. Otherwise it might be directly submitted for assessment. If considered in a full meeting, it is often a good idea to let the heads of the small team present the part of the final report they researched earlier. This keeps them happy and involved (job satisfaction!) and as the detailed experts they will be able to handle questions better than the overall leader anyway.

SO WHAT COULD GO WRONG IN GROUP PROJECTS?

Despite the many benefits you can gain from undertaking a group project, they often require more effort than ordinary assignments. The following are some of the problems that can arise and which you should look out for.

General problems
- Problems of authority and control versus democratic participation may arise if the overall leader proves to be unpopular.
- Differences in political or social views can sometimes make compromise difficult; fanatics need to be sidelined.
- The progress of the whole group can be no faster than its slowest part; you are the weakest link!
- You will probably have to learn new (and valuable) skills but this takes time.

Coordination problems
- Within each small team, some individuals will probably be slower than others, which holds things up and tends to irritate the faster workers.
- There will probably be quality differences between the reports from the small groups.
- The report of one small team may clash in some way with the report of another – the overall group leader can now bring into play the political skills of mediation and compromise when he or she gets together with the team leaders.
- Some individuals may object to the thrust or conclusions of their own group's draft report – solving this problem requires the same skills.
- One or more small teams may put their report in late.

Poor leader problems
If the person you initially chose turns out to be hopeless, it can be painful to try to move them out and replace them with someone you hope will be better. There is a lot of face involved, and it may be easier to live with a poor leader and provide support by means of a small advisory group – who might in fact have to do some of the real work.

The allocating marks problem
The final report will receive a mark which should be a percentage. Let us assume this is 80 per cent and all groups receive this. It is easy and tempting to give equal marks (in this case 80 per cent) to the individual members of the group or small team. If this is done, that is the end of it. However, some individuals will have taken on more responsibility and done more to organise, control, write, and liaise than others. They will probably feel they should get more marks, and this does seem fair.

It is possible to give different members different marks to reflect their efforts. For example, if there are five members of a group, there are (5 x 80) notional marks to allocate, or 400. As an example, one member might get 95 per cent, one get 65 per cent and the other three get 80 per cent. This would have to be discussed and agreed by the team, which can prove embarrassing. Once you move away from equal marks for all, there is no guarantee of an easy solution when sorting out what seems a fair distribution. Interestingly enough, at one time this was an issue for those working in teams in communist countries using central planning.

The free-rider problem
One or two people may sign up for the course, turn up once or twice, then after that do little work, yet expect to get an equal share of the marks. This is not only unfair, it is resented by those who worked hard and who carried these slackers. There always seems to be the odd drone among the worker bees. If you have a tough leader or group then you might choose to penalise them, maybe even give them a failing grade. Often, however, people are not that hard, or feel sorry for one or more of the individuals concerned. If spotted early enough, their own small team leader could have a word with them to try to get them to do more, but in my experience it rarely seems to work. Peer group pressure could be tried but such people are often impervious. Well, at least you can ensure that everyone knows who these free-riders are.

In the short term free-riders appear to win: they get marks for little or no work. In the medium term it is the other way round: they become losers. They get a bad reputation, lose friends, and of course they learn little about the subject matter. In the long term they are even worse off: they fail to develop the skills they need and life will be a lot harder once they start that job – and their promotion may well be slow. Being a free-rider may be tempting, but if you care about yourself, it's a no-no.

CASE STUDIES

Aziz is a good team leader
Aziz is very good at group work – he is chosen as the overall leader and naturally is part of one small team as well. He opts to be an ordinary member, not the leader of the team, but he takes over when the leader is ill for a week and somehow keeps the position. He manages to diffuse a situation where two small team leaders were at loggerheads and succeeds in keeping them both happy. He writes up the overall report on his own and gives it to two others to edit and, although he finds it hard to admit, he discovers that this actually does improve it.

Betty learns how to work in a team
Betty is used to working on her own and despite benefitting from having found a study-buddy (who has finally asked her out), she lacks the skills

to work well with others. She is a poor group performer at first and finds it hard to trust the other members to do their bit properly, and rather wishes to hog the work. She does well, going off on her own to dig up information, and the notes she puts into the team are excellent – but she cannot argue persuasively in the discussions. Her team members know how well she scores in essay writing and she is talked into writing up her team findings, which she does ably. She feels happy about that and has begun to feel that she belongs in the team. She also makes several new friends out of the experience.

Charlie enjoys being part of a team
Charlie does surprisingly well. Early on he was tempted to laze around and be a free-rider but he actually got interested in the topic and ended up working hard with several of his friends. When some of his suggestions were adopted he felt particularly good about it. He is beginning to think he might join a study-group if team work can be fun like this, and it certainly makes learning less painful for him. For this reason, he probably got more out of the group project than anyone.

DISCUSSION POINTS

1. What sort of job would you like after you graduate? What skills can you gain from participating in team projects that would help you get that job and later succeed well in it?

2. Have you ever worked on a team project or with a partner before? Did you research separately or together? Did you write up separately or together? What did you learn from the experience? Would you do it differently next time?

3. If you had the problem of a free-rider in a group project, can you think of a way to tackle it? Do any other possibilities come to mind? Which of these ways would you try first?

SUMMARY

- Get involved in a group project if you can – the skills you develop will serve you well in life.
- At the first session, choose a leader, get an outline adopted if you can, and make a timetable.
- Set up several small teams, probably one for each section of the outline.
- Each team researches a clearly defined area and reports up.
- The leader and a few others put together a draft report that has to be agreed.
- The final report is written and then approved by all, probably in full session, before submission.
- Problems of a poor leader, tricky coordination, and free-riders may arise.
- Group projects need work and time – but the pay-off is well worth it and they are fun too.

10. Role-playing and drama queens – presentation matters

LIFE, THE UNIVERSE AND EVERYTHING: DEVELOPING MORE SKILLS THAT WILL STAND YOU IN GOOD STEAD

As part of your university career, you should seriously consider trying to do one or more subjects that involve role-playing. These are often located in the university's commerce or business faculty, and many universities now allow you to take such courses whatever your main study area. Check the university handbook or ask in the department or faculty office what's available in your institution.

☺ Our speaker does not intend to bore you with a long speech...he can ☺
easily do it with a short one.

Role-playing presentations can be immense fun and are often a superior version of primary school show-and-tell; but now it's for grown-ups. You are moving from the page to the stage; putting it another way, you are no longer writing an essay but engaging in course encounters of the word kind. Programmes that include role-play require a bit more effort because you have to work on both the content and the presentation for top marks, but they're worth it and moreover they are enjoyable.

What's in it for me? Good question! You will develop the skill to
- Research a practical project, which is dear to the heart of those hiring in business and government.
- Develop your own individual approach to a problem.
- Improve your communication abilities.
- Enhance your self-confidence and learn to think on your feet.
- Organise complex material in new ways and explain them to an audience.
- Work out creative methods of using props in making a presentation.
- Put together a visually attractive and persuasive final report.
- Sell yourself, and persuade people to your point of view.

In short, role-playing sessions develop your vocational skills, look brilliant on your CV, provide you with an interesting topic to raise in a job interview, and can really give you the edge. If you get the opportunity for a role-playing course, go for it!

Don't reinvent the wheel – learn from the others
It is tempting not to go to the presentations of your fellow students, when you still have heaps of work to do, are struggling to define your topic clearly, and searching for elusive information. Resist this temptation! You should attend everybody else's sessions and watch, listen and learn from their strengths and weaknesses. Consider carefully whatever criticisms and suggestions the staff member makes to them and see how you can incorporate this into the delivery you are yet to make. More marks for you!

Unlike tutorials, if you have a choice it is better to do your presentation late in the term because by then you will have learned a lot from simply watching the others.

DEALING WITH ESSENTIALS: THE BUCK STARTS HERE

Timing
Make sure you know how long you have got in which to make your presentation. There will almost certainly be time taken out at the end for questions, discussion, and suggestions. Typically, an hour session might

have 20 minutes for your actual presentation, but in a half-hour session you would be lucky to get more than 12 minutes or so.

Get there early on the day
Try to be there in good time so you can check out the room, make sure all the equipment you need is there, is working and you know how to handle it. You can also lay out any props you will use, and put up any maps, posters, or photographs that you intend to point to. You might want to look at the timetable or check in the departmental office to see if the room will be in use before your session. If this is the case, you may have to set up some wall stuff well in advance.

Dressing the part
You need to dress up in character to get your best performance: it will help you to do better and will also impress the student audience and staff member (better marks!). In most cases men should wear a dark suit and tie with a light-coloured shirt; women a dark business suit or plain blouse and dark skirt, and both need leather shoes – the whole power-dressing game in fact. Women should use make-up and simple jewellery like earrings – it all helps. Of course, if you are going to be a historian acting the part of a Baron who is supposed to persuade King John to accept the Magna Carta, your dress choice is perhaps more limited.

You need to stand up straight during your performance (yep, it's a performance), with your shoulders back, stomach in and chin up – but try to avoid the ultra rigid "soldier on parade" stance; it merely tends to make you look dumb.

Use cards to present your talk
Do not write an essay and read it out – when making a presentation this is a recipe for a low-grade result. Instead, put your notes on cards (which takes care of the problem of what to do with one hand) and glance at them for your next point. Keep your head up and go for maximum eye contact; keep sweeping the room, looking in a person's eyes for a second or two, and make sure you have eventually looked in everybody's eyes at least once. Keep the cards low and do not hold them up in front of your face. It's best not to place them on something, such as a lectern, and then read from them, as this tends to point the top of your head at the audience and

prevents eye contact. You can of course gesture with the cards to emphasise points you are making.

LET THE TALKING BEGIN

Setting the scene
Start by telling the audience who you are, who they are, why they are here, what you want from them in general terms, and the title of your project. If your instructions do not state who the members of the audience are supposed to be, you decide and tell them anyway. This gets them involved and starts a bit of bonding going. Only when the scene is set should you begin your talk proper.

Starting the presentation
A good way is to pass out your handout. Make sure that your name, the project title, the date, and who the audience is supposed to be are on the front page. And the staff member's name too is a good idea as it makes them feel included rather than ignored. A good logo helps a lot – either design your own or use a computer to import a suitable graphic, perhaps from the Internet. When passing out any material, make sure that if there is a leader of the group in the audience (the managing director of a company, the leader of a delegation, the President of Ruritania etc.), they get the item first – well, after the staff guy anyway (the one who will decide your mark). In your particular course, you might find the staff member is automatically the leader.

☺ Q. How many psychiatrists does it take to change a light-bulb? ☺
A. Only one – but the bulb must really want to change.

Grabbing the audience quickly
Try to grab their attention at once, perhaps by some bold statement ("In the next ten minutes I hope to persuade you to invest 30 million pounds in a laboratory in Doncaster.") or by drawing their attention to a particularly impressive poster or overhead transparency. A prop can help a lot; e.g. if you plan to produce and market doughnuts you might bring some real ones along for people – hold one up as soon as you can and show it as a "teaser" – and tell them that they can have a bite or two to try at the end. Such things add interest, get the attention of the audience, and earn marks for you.

YES, THEY'RE ALL LOOKING AT YOU!

You will be standing out in front. Watch your posture and remember to stand tall and look dominant.

Things to avoid
- Putting one or both hands in your pockets.
- Putting your hands in front of your face and partially obscuring it.
- Leaning on the furniture.
- Keeping your arms hanging permanently by your sides.
- Keeping your hands permanently behind your back.
- Standing with your arms on your hips.
- Clenching your fists.
- Scratching yourself – some people itch when nervous!
- Biting your lips or twisting your hair.
- Brushing specks off your clothes.

What sort of gesture will you make this time?
You need to use gestures to put your points over. What to do with your hands is a perennial problem and it is easy to look silly. As early in the term as you can, start watching speakers on TV, including politicians, game-show presenters and entertainers; notice what they do with their hands and arms. Look for particular gestures that accompany good news; underline a point to be emphasised; attempt to persuade; or try to diminish criticism. You can practise these in front of a mirror, first in silence and then while speaking. After all, the TV people you are learning from already did this! This is a good life skill to possess.

Be aware of the way you use your voice – keep checking as you talk
Refer back to the advice on using your voice in Chapter 6, page 90.

You're not in space: try hard to ensure your screams are heard
Make sure that everyone can hear you. Project your voice so that those in the back row have no problems listening. If there is a microphone, try to keep it the same distance from your mouth as you talk. If you get a

question from the side, don't forget to move the mike as you turn your head or your voice might fade. If the microphone is fixed in one spot, remember not to move away from it when you speak; and if you have turned away to take a question, do not forget to return to the mike to answer.

Avoiding nervous speech habits
As in the case of presenting an oral, you can ask your friends if you have any bad speech habits – almost everyone seems to have some. In particular avoid incomprehensible noises like "errr", "erm" or "um", and punctuating your sentences with words such as "yeah?", "you know", "right", "like", "so", "OK?" or "innit?". If you have such a habit, it annoys people and they may start to listen for the noises (and even start to count them), rather than to your message. Remember however that the deliberate use of phrases like "Right then!" or "So where do we go from here?" can be effective in marking the change to a new section, focusing the interest of the audience on something important, or waking up any individuals nodding off.

Repeating points for emphasis
If a point is really important and you wish to emphasise it, you can repeat the phrase when you are speaking in public: "We expect to earn thirty-five per cent by year two – that's thirty-five per cent!" Notice how many politicians use this trick when speaking in public. You must not use such repetition in a written essay of course.

VISUAL AIDS – ALWAYS GIVE THEM SOMETHING TO FOCUS ON

Overhead transparencies: an OHT can be HOT
OHTs are virtually essential these days in universities, although in the real world the use of computer presentation packages such as PowerPoint often replaces them.

Prepare all your OHTs in advance and make sure the font you use is large enough. I personally think it is a good idea to use block capitals unless you have a specific reason not to – these are only the equivalent of shouting when in email messages. If you choose to go with lower case, make the font bigger than 12 point, which is often the word processor's default size. In my experience, more OHTs fail to work properly through the text being too small than for any other reason.

The sort of things you can put on your OHTs
- Your talk outline – it's good if you can get it on one OHT.
- If you supply your outline as a handout, never duplicate it with an identical OHT as this looks silly and redundant.
- All the data you need and will refer to.
- Any systems or flow charts you will use.
- All the diagrams you will use.
- Perhaps maps, photographs, plans or blueprints, depending on your topic.

Tips for using OHTs
- Use a word processor and printer to make your OHTs; do not use handwriting.
- Remember to spell-check each OHT: silly errors are easy to make and miss, but the audience will definitely notice.
- Enlarge all your data if you photocopied it from a book or journal, otherwise it will be too small to be read easily by those at the back.
- Only put up the bits of data you actually need, not huge tables containing heaps of figures that you will never mention.
- It is better not to put up a complex diagram in the first few minutes, it can frighten people – keep the first one simple. But later in your talk you might use more complicated graphs, diagrams and pictures to communicate information. By then you should have grabbed your audience and they will be interested enough to make the effort.
- Once an OHT is up on the screen, leave it there! People need a long time to absorb things.
- Do not keep turning the machine on and off – leave it on with your last OHT showing or else put your outline up again.
- Remember the data never explain themselves – tell us what they mean.
- Colour me successful! For straight text you can use black on a white background. For other things, such as diagrams, you should use colour; you can underline, highlight, or draw boxes, circles or arrows as you need; three colours are usually enough. Do not use background colours on OHTs unless you have a special reason; green (not too dark) for an environmental issue might work well, for example.

- Do not change the colours unless you have a reason; and then say what that is.
- Best avoid green with red; orange with yellow; orange with brown; blue with green. They can be hard for some people to distinguish. Incidentally, did you know that very few women are colour blind but it is common in men? So in an all-women's college you might be OK.
- Black goes with yellow or red but not with blue; red goes well with yellow; white text on a blue background appeals to some – but perhaps not many.
- You will need a "key" to explain the meaning of your different colours.
- Use a marker pen to number your OHTs in the order you will use them – you'll be glad you did this when you drop the slippery things all over the floor.
- If you actually need to draw on an OHT as you are talking (perhaps shove in an arrow to point to something special) you can easily do so by sliding the OHT under the transparent roll on the machine or a blank transparency; then you can draw on *that*. This keeps the OHT unmarked for when you want to use it again later.

Using the OHT machine

- Well ahead of time ensure the room has a machine and that it is working properly.
- Make sure you know how to work and focus that particular machine.
- Do not stand in front of the beam.
- Do not block the view of the screen for some in the audience; keep moving to one side if necessary.

Black – and whiteboards

If you have a choice, always use OHTs not blackboards or whiteboards; to use those you have to turn your back on the audience. This could be dangerous in some institutions, but more importantly it is then harder for people to hear you and you have lost eye contact.

Make sure you have the right pens or chalk
Check in advance to see if there is chalk (coloured if you need it) or proper whiteboard pens and an eraser. If not, take your own. Check that the pens are designed for whiteboards, because many pens intended for other purposes will not rub out; this not only irritates the university but you will also run out of space quickly.

Write larger than normal
Write clearly using large letters to ensure the people at the back can read it easily. Try to keep your lines straight, and if using a blackboard, please do not make the chalk squeak!

Speak up!
When you turn your back to write, or to indicate something on the board, remember to turn your head sideways and project your voice more, because much of the sound disappears when you are not facing your audience.

Using video films
A short video film can be effective as long as it is central to your project. If it is long or peripheral it will be a sad waste of your limited time.

> ☺ It's not when they walk out you should worry; it's when they stand up ☺
> and walk towards you.

USING PROPS

You must use some props if you are to be fully effective. They grab people's attention, increase their interest and make them want to listen to you.

Some tips about props
- If you can, it's usually better to use actual items themselves: a toy, dress material, food, whatever is appropriate.
- If you cannot get hold of the real thing you can use representations of such items, e.g. photographs, posters, handbills, or pictures.
- Use your props as early as you can – a teaser particularly can work well; as an example, you could show the audience a prop early on but only use it fully later.

- Try to get audience participation if you can; e.g. pass a prop round for them to taste, stroke, or examine. This works well with small groups of, say, fifteen but is much less effective with huge audiences, as the items will not go all the way round in time.

MORE ROLE-PLAYING TIPS

Staying in character
Once you begin, do not drop out of character. Even if a close friend asks you a question, stay with your professional voice and manner.

Adopting a particular style in your approach
Consider the best type of presentation for you.
- "Warm, knowledgeable and helpful" works well for many – it is good for extroverts.
- "Cool, clear and scientific" is suitable for some – the quiet, the introvert, or those who are nervous may do better with this one.
- "Friendly and amusing" is only for the few who are naturally witty.
- "Shallow and superficial" – there is a real danger of drifting into this if you try for "Friendly and amusing" and it breaks down.
- "Diffident and uncertain" is always a bad style.

Whatever approach you go for, appearing confident helps a lot, as does deep sincerity. Once you have learned to fake that there will be no stopping you.

Coping with accidents
If you drop something like an OHT or a prop, what can you do?
- Ignore it – this often works well.
- Turn it to your advantage with a quick and witty remark – almost always the best way if you can do it. ("Whoops, one is escaping!" or "Clearly that one isn't quite dead yet!")
- Stumble an apology and look remorseful. This is never a good idea, especially if you are naturally diffident, because it makes you look truly incompetent.
- Grovel around and pick it up? This can irritate if people are forced to wait for you, so avoid it if you can, especially if it rolled away.

- If you really need to use it later, you will have to pick it up as neatly and quickly as possible. A mature student might find a remark like "This is not helping my lumbago one little bit!" goes down well.

Coping with jocular remarks — the hecklers
It is usually best to totally ignore any teasing remarks from friends; a fierce glare from you might help to stop them. Only if you are witty and experienced at humorous put-downs should you think of responding. Otherwise a poor reply is embarrassing, leaves a bad taste in the mouth, you will have to work hard to regain the audience, and it can earn you a lower mark.

If you have the kind of slack friends who actually do this, try not to look at the staff member for help, as it will weaken your presentation and your image. Oh, and as a last extreme you might consider hanging out with a few different guys in the future.

Stressing the positive points of your product or your project
It is best not to knock your competitors by name, whether these are companies, countries, political parties or alternative theories. It will probably irritate some of those present, and in the real world the word might easily get back to the opposition! Besides, generally you do not wish to give any publicity to them by naming rival products. It is far better to stress in what way your item, theory or policy etc. is simply preferable. At the early planning stage, it is worth spending time thinking about how you can best promote your cause. When you have left Uni and have a paid job, this particular skill can help you a lot.

Measuring success
As well as explaining what you are aiming to do, you should decide how you will measure success in your particular project. You might well be asked this as a question later, even if it is not a part of your presentation. It can be tricky figuring this one out, but at least try to be prepared just in case some evil alien creature tries to trap you with this one.

Good words and phrases to use
Select words that sound positive and encouraging (see Figure 10, page 152). Notice that fashionable phrases come and go, so that not all of these

suggestions might be desirable a decade hence, and new ones will surely arise.

What's in it for me?
Another question that will be high in the mind of your audience is "what do I get out of it?" Make sure you address that question as you go through your presentation. Either near the very beginning or towards the end are good times to cover this. Depending on the nature of your project it might be things like winning the election, making more money, expanding market share... whatever.

Figure 10. Some good words and phrases to use – but choose what is suitable for your particular discipline and project

Active participation	Potential
Dynamic	Rewarding
Exciting prospects	Safe
Growth area	Stimulating
Long experience	Strategic
Opportunity	Strong probabilities
Popular	Valuable

Using positive language
Negative phrases are best avoided, so try to find a substitute if you can. The aim is to be positive and sound as if you are in charge of events. If you are ever forced to admit ignorance, immediately say what you will do to correct this, e.g. "I will find out and get the answer to you by close of business today". Notice the positive tone (see Figure 11 for some examples).

Your concluding sentences
Your final words should sum up the project and remind the audience what exactly you want from them. It is polite to thank them for their attendance and attention. Then ask for questions if that is the norm for your course.

THAT IMPORTANT QUESTION TIME IN ROLE-PLAYING SESSIONS

Here is where you can shine, but it helps if you have self-confidence – that time you spent having fun in the drama society can now pay off! I hope by now that you have thought about the possible questions they might ask and have prepared some sort of answer to them.

Figure 11. Some negative phrases with preferred positive substitutes

Negative phrases to avoid	Positive substitutes
I don't know	I will find out; all the data is not yet in but it seems as if...; my assistant is looking at that right now.
Maybe; Perhaps; Could be	It certainly looks that way; we currently think that is the case; apparently; we suspect that...
I think you are wrong	It is too soon to be certain but it looks as if...; the data actually suggest ...
I guess so	Yes; that's right!; absolutely!; all the data we have so far show you are correct.
I am trying to...	I will
I think it was called....	With a name like...
I have never been there (as an excuse)	All my research indicates...
Somewhere around there (pointing to a map)	Just here (pointing to the map)
Somebody told me	It is believed in the industry...
I've read in a book; I read somewhere	I believe; some suggest; one source indicated...

Look at the actual questioner
Never look worried by the question. Get eye contact at once, look pleased, try to be positive and seem interested in the question. Remember not to look at the staff member when you get a question, because it looks as if you are seeking help or sympathy, and may be in a bit of a panic.

Buying time
If it is a tricky question that you had not anticipated, you can try to buy time and make the questioner feel good with stalling phrases (see Chapter 6, page 97). An occasional slight pause while you think (say two or three seconds) is acceptable and it shows you are really considering the issue carefully. You cannot do this for every question though or it will tend to make you look dumb!

Using humour
If you are capable, you not only can but should use humour in your answer. This is often not a good idea in seminars, but it often works well in role-playing sessions, as well as before large audiences.

☺   Very funny Scotty, now beam up my clothes.   ☺

Using your props at question time
When answering a question, pick up and use a prop if it would be appropriate. It interests the audience, impresses the staff member, and can be useful to deflect attention from the quality of your answer if it is weak! However, do be careful not to fiddle with any of them unconsciously.

CASE STUDIES

Aziz makes an excellent presentation
Aziz did well in a project concerned with establishing a medical clinic in a Third World country using overseas aid. He prepared a good handout and several OHTs using colour and originality of design. He dressed up properly in a suit and tie – and his drama talents showed. He immediately grabbed the audience using a plastic skull and a poster of a baby to talk about life expectancy. He used several interesting props, including a couple of medical implements his wife could borrow from the hospital where she works part-time. He enjoyed the session and so did the audience; he got a top mark of A++.

Betty learns a lot from the experience
Betty did well despite her fears – she attended all the early presentations and listened to the suggestions of the staff member. Her project was about selling education in Britain to overseas students as a form of export earning. She prepared her handout and chose her props well. Her OHTs were well-drawn and neat. She dressed up for it but her general lack of interest in clothes meant that she looked a bit dowdy. She used make-up which helped, but her diffidence showed in her low quiet voice, and she found herself unable to look at individuals in the audience. The process terrified her but a sympathetic tutor gave her a decent B++. She learned a lot and feels next time she would do better and might get an A. She has begun to acquire new skills that she rather desperately needs, and actually got more from the role-playing course than anyone.

Not making any effort means low marks
Charlie's project was about starting a new political party in Wales aimed at fighting the next general election. His presentation was not particularly good and he did not go to many of the earlier sessions. His handout had spelling errors and he forgot to put his name on it. His OHTs however were attractive and well designed with good colour, which impressed the assessor, but he failed to use any props. He wore a jacket and tie but his ancient trainers rather spoiled the effect. He learned a bit from the process of presentation, and got a mark of C.

DISCUSSION POINTS

1. What sort of stance and gestures would not look good in a role-playing session? Do you tend to drift into using any of these? What can you do with your hands when speaking in public?

2. Quickly think of a project in your discipline or area. What really interesting first sentence can you invent to grab the attention of the audience? Can you think of two props you could use for this project?

3. Think up a list of unsuitable words (i.e. that can give a negative image) and good words (a positive image) for Aziz's, Betty's and Charlie's projects:
A) Raising the money to build a medical clinic in a third world country.
B) Selling education in Britain to overseas students.
C) Attempting to set up a new political party in Wales.

(This particular exercise can help to improve your essay writing by forcing you to think carefully about what you wish to say and the best words to convey your thoughts.)

SUMMARY

- Give your session late in the term if possible.
- Dress up for a better performance and marks.
- Work on your stance and gestures for a good performance.
- Always make your presentation from notes rather than reading it out.
- Set the scene, pass out handouts, and grab the audience at once.
- With OHTs make them large, use colour where appropriate, and leave them up.
- Props are essential: things often work better than pictures – but data and figures may need to be put into graphs or charts to be understood.
- Pay attention to detail and stay in character.
- Decide how you will cope if you drop something.
- Emphasise the strong points of your product etc., rather than criticise your rivals or the opposition.
- Always use positive language.
- When handling questions ignore the staff member, get eye contact with the questioner, and use humour and props if you can.
- The skills you are learning here will benefit you throughout your life.

11. End of part one: the homecoming

THE END OF YOUR FIRST TERM

Home is where you lay your hat and maybe a few close friends

The old town may look the same but your friends may appear different
When you go home for Christmas after your first term away, the town you remember fondly may feel small and perhaps even a bit boring. You might wonder what you saw in some of the friends you left behind and, like Muggles, they might seem parochial, small-minded, and not as interesting as some of your new friends at college. If you are the first from your family or circle to go to university this is a probability rather than a possibility.

A voyage round your parents
Your parents will quite likely seem older than you remember them; you have been surrounded by young people and haven't seen your immediate ancestors for a while. They may perhaps be unable to understand what you are doing, how you spend your time, and why on earth you are interested in all these crazy new things. Be prepared for questions about what you do at university – but do not be surprised if your parents quickly lose interest when you try to explain. What you are seeing is partly a reflection of the changes in yourself. You are growing up and the changes in you are beginning to show; but as a homecoming experience it can all be a little unsettling. If you're lucky they won't ask or else will understand.

Your pet probably remembers you clearly and you will be pleased to meet up again, although you really cannot rely on reptiles. But because love is a four-legged word it is more likely you have a more normal kind of pet who will probably be delighted to see you again.

☺ Does my asp look big in this? ☺

After you get home
First you will probably need to relax, take a break from studying, and have fun. It's OK to be home and deranged. Later, if you can face it, it is a good idea to do some preparatory reading for next term. If you make a crude timetable of what you want to do, or write down the names of a book or two you intend to read, it might strengthen your resolution. It is tempting to spend the whole vacation enjoying yourself, but if you can bear to put aside a few days to do some preparation work, you will feel the benefit next year. If you are working on a vacation job for the entire period, I sympathise. Try to get a minimum of ten days off to rest and restore your batteries before you go back. For the rest of your time at college you can keep on pursuing the good study habits that you have learned and develop new ones where you can. It will be useful to read this book now and again, to remind yourself of what you should be doing and reinforce your motivation.

TOWARDS THE END OF YOUR FIRST-YEAR

Having survived your first-year it is not a bad idea to take stock and consider how you look now; for, since you came to university, you have changed more than you might imagine. This self-examination process can boost your confidence, help with your motivation to study, and perhaps show you where you could make improvements next year.

Assessing experience
You might want to set aside an evening on your own to think about it and make a list of:
- What you have learned academically in broad terms.

- The marks you received in different assessment items.
- The skills you have begun to develop.
- The new experiences you have had.
- The new places you have been.
- The new friends you have made.
- The problems you have encountered and how you've coped.
- The areas where you can improve, e.g. the split between study-time and work.
- The state of your emotional life and personal relationships – do any changes need to be made?

Check the list, pat yourself on the back for the good parts and think about how you could improve in the less-than-good areas. Then make a second list. On this write down what you will do better next year – this is your "Second-Year Resolution" list. Put it in a safe place and dig it out when you come back next term. This process can help improve your motivation.

☺ Free advice costs you nothing – until you act upon it when it can prove really expensive. Congratulate yourself that your decision to buy this book was a good investment! ☺

The looming second-year – what now?

Your first-year notes
It might seem tempting to throw out or even enjoy a celebratory bonfire of some or all of your first-year notes that you think you will never need again – do not do this! You can never be sure what you will need in the future. You will kick yourself for having to look up in books something you once had good notes on.

Housing
If you were lucky enough to get into university accommodation, you might have to move out at the end of the first-year. If you can stay a second-year, the good news is that you normally will not have to pay for the period you are away. You might, however, have to pack up your stuff and store it in a trunk or suitcase somewhere in the building. Universities often play at Rent-a-Room during the vacation in order to make money from tourists and other strangers.

Sorting out next year's accommodation
Assuming you have to move out, late in your first-year think about your friends and decide who you could stand to share with. They are quite likely to be different from the ones you made long ago in Fresher Week! You can then approach your chosen few on a casual basis to gauge their response. You need to sort out how many bedrooms you require, the area you want to be in (a list in order of preference might help when you come to the great search), and the maximum rent that you can afford (and see "Choosing where to live", page 10). Check the adverts in the local paper so that you get some idea of what you will have to pay or talk to an estate agent in the area you would like to be. Less desirable places may be standing empty now but better ones may take around 4–8 weeks to become available.

If you are approached to share with others, it might be a good idea to stall and ask for a couple of days to think it over. This will give you time to consider the people you would have to live with next term.

☺ In your new place it's best to avoid spring cleaning: it's too ☺
difficult getting them back in the mattress.

Avoid paying a retainer
If you have been living in private accommodation it is often best to give it up rather than pay for the months when you will not be using it. You could ask your dear landlord to keep it for you without a retainer but it would be unusual to get such an agreement. If you decide to leave, you might have to pay a bit more for a new place next year, but the difference in rent will probably be less than a retainer would be, often significantly so. By now you will have more idea of what to look for anyway, based on your experiences, and might fancy a change.

Checking out the second-year courses
You might have to make a decision about which subjects or courses you will study next year, especially if you are doing one of the newer modular degrees. This choice should not be rushed. It is a good idea to get advice from your tutor, from any staff member you know, and by talking to second-year or third-year students. Your university handbook may have a list of the courses on offer, but at best there will be bald descriptions with no indication of how good each course is. Check to see if your student union has organised student evaluation of courses. The comments are

often fascinatingly scurrilous, and will give you a much better idea of how interesting and well taught the courses are. If they say a course is "popular", "interesting", or "fun", this is attractive; but remember that "challenging", "stimulating", or "difficult but valuable" may offer better long-term prospects. If they say "It's rubbish" be very careful. Your choice! If they have not yet done a survey, suggest they might. You can point out it could help their CVs.

Choosing your subjects – even monarchs don't get that chance
When selecting what subjects to study, your main decision is between what interests you and what you think would appeal to an employer when you look for a job. Other than for posts requiring specific skills, like vets or accountants, many employers prefer to choose a quality student who has demonstrated ability by scoring good marks in whatever courses he or she has done. Employers know that a good person can always be trained to their particular needs. You can usually get a good job more easily if you have an upper second or first class degree, as these indicate diligence and intelligence. A bare pass in subjects that relate directly to the industry concerned may be less attractive to the one doing the hiring. Most people tend to score best at things that they enjoy, so you may be better off choosing courses and subjects that interest you, rather than picking what you think an employer might want but that you will hate to study. Yeah! It's a tricky one!

Thinking about the job skills you will need
Remember, it is in your interest to develop transferable skills, such as a good communication capacity; the ability to solve problems; the facility to cooperate with others in a team; the knack of organising tasks in priority order; and the expertise to manage your time properly. If you took part in a team project or role-playing session in your first-year you have made a good start and should try to do more such courses if you can. As with most things, you get better with practice. You might check to see if your university offers courses that directly teach such skills too.

When you come to apply for jobs, these abilities should be displayed in a prominent place on your CV. They not only impress, they also provide a good talking point at interviews and it gives you something valuable to say when asked those awful mind-numbing questions like "What benefits do you think you got from going to university?"; "Tell us, what are your strengths?"; "Why would you like to work for our firm?"; "What do you think you have to offer our company?"; or "Is there anything you would like to ask or tell us?"

When selecting your second-year courses, it's helpful to take a quick look at the later ones too
You might also check out the third-year courses in your university handbook to see if there are prerequisites for any that you might be interested in doing. Sometimes you have to choose carefully in the second-year to avoid being barred from something brilliant in the third.

Getting your book list
Once you have settled what you want to do, see if you can get next year's book list from the lecturer or the office. If you have the time, you could look at the set textbook during the vacation. If you decide early enough, you could ask your local home-town library to order the book – if you attend a university away from home, your parents could do this in advance for you. If you can renew online, you might even be able to hang onto it for your own use next term. Saves you buying!

Best not to book in advance
It is best not to purchase a second-year textbook while still in your first-year in case you change your mind and do a different subject. You can't trust those swine the staff not to change the textbook in the interim either!

Studying in your second-year
A trap to avoid as you prepare for your second-year is the temptation to slacken off. This is a dangerous time: you feel completely at home at university and the end is well out of sight (unlike for third-year students for whom the clock is ticking and the bell will soon toll). It is easy to revel in the apparent freedom, over-indulge in socialising, and suffer reduced marks. This is a particular danger for those moving out of university accommodation into sharing a house with others. The cry of "It's party time!" is particularly seductive.

Reasons to be cheerful, part one!
Next year will be even better. As a seasoned student you can enjoy the spice of life. You are an old hand now, and will shortly have a new intake of Freshers to consider as a different and perhaps slightly inferior species. You also have two more years to have a wicked time as you enjoy a great

way to live. It's a once-in-a-lifetime opportunity just being there! Enjoy it! The second-year is fantastic – you know your way around and the final exams are still a long way off.

But sooner than you might think you will be getting both of these:

So don't slacken off too much!

☺ May you earn enough in life to test the proposition that money does ☺
not make a person happy.

CASE STUDIES

Aziz decides how he can improve

Aziz thinks about what he has done over the year and determines to tackle his weak spots, which are mainly in essay writing, and he recognises that he has a touch of arrogance. He has done well in team and role-playing and this pulls his overall mark up to a most respectable A. He is steadily improving and is looking forward to his second-year. He chooses next year's courses with an eye on the banking job he has now decided that he wants, including one course that he feels sounds boring. He may be storing up trouble here, as gaining a good mark in this subject will be hard for him. Thankfully, he has no housing problem to consider and his wife is still supportive.

Betty's careful choice of course will pay off

Betty carefully goes over the year and correctly decides that diffidence is still a weakness and boosting her self-confidence is the main area where she can improve. She decides she will find a study-group and also she and her study-buddy (now her steady boy-friend) intend to join the drama society together next term. This will certainly help her to gain self-assurance. She looked into next year's courses and consulted the students' union guide. She is generally selecting subjects that sound interesting and challenging and has deliberately picked on one with a major oral presentation component so that she can carry on improving her presentation skills. She is still living with her parents but is starting to think that it might be good to spread her wings and share a house before too long.

Charlie takes little care in choosing his courses

Charlie did not even think of summing up his year and just wants to get home. He is relieved to have scraped through to second-year. Next term he intends to share a house with four other students and thinks it will be fun. He is unaware though that he might have to struggle even more against the temptation to go out socialising and drinking. He chooses his second-year courses quickly and only bothers to do this because he is forced to fill in a form. He chooses those whose titles sound easy, and one that someone told him was OK, but he didn't check this with anyone else. As a result, his overall selection is a bit of a mishmash. He is also in for a shock next year, because one of the subjects he chooses needs a lot of maths and he doesn't know this yet. He might find that he will have to drop it and find something else that he can do. The dark side of nowhere is starting to beckon, but he can, if he is prepared to put in a lot more effort, still get that degree he wants.

DISCUSSION POINTS

1. What subjects have you enjoyed most during the year? Which the least? Can you work out why that is? What does this suggest for your choice of subjects in the second-year?

2. What skills have you developed over the year? Which area do you think is most in need of improvement?

3. If you have to move into new accommodation next year, what exactly will you be looking for? With whom will you share? In which area(s) of town would you prefer to live? Have you checked prices and the transport facilities carefully? Are there empty places or will there be a few weeks' wait before you can move in?

SUMMARY

- Be prepared to notice some differences when you go home.
- Make a list of what you have achieved and another list of what you can do to improve.
- If renting privately it is often best to give up your accommodation for the vacation, unless you are happily settled in. Do the sums carefully first.
- If you need to share accommodation next year, choose the people carefully.
- Think long and hard about the area you would like to live in and the maximum rent you can pay.
- Check out the second-year courses, try to choose what interests you, but keep an eye on your future career.
- Ask in the student union if they have done course appraisals of the second-year.
- When selecting courses remember that those involving skills of communication, problem-solving, and team work can help you get a good job.
- If you act as leader on a group project, make sure it goes on your CV – it gives you something interesting to talk about at the interview and impresses the guy hiring.
- Try to get a book list for your chosen courses and do some preliminary reading for next year if you can face it.
- Beware of the danger of slackening off in the second-year.

AND HEY! ENJOY THE REST OF YOUR TIME AT UNI!

===================================

If you have found this book useful, check out "Bucknall's Refuge" for other books and pieces by the author, some of them free: www.bucknall.homestead.com Should the URL change by the time you read this, you can use your browser to search for "Bucknall's Refuge" and find it in its new home.

===================================

Appendix A. Some useful Internet URLs

Alt.comp.freeware A site that discusses good freeware computer programs which is well worth checking out. If you like a commercial package but are short of cash, see if there is a free substitute. http://groups.google.co.uk/group/alt.comp.freeware?lnk=gschg&hl=en

Ask the Econsultant. An excellent list of freeware sorted by what you want to do. http://www.econsultant.com/i-want-freeware-utilities/

Dogpile. An online meta-search engine. http://www.dogpile.com/

Freecycle. This is an international organisation that allows people to give away things they no longer need. If you are setting up house, it's a good place to look or advertise. See http://freecycle.org/ for your area.

Freewarewiki.com. An excellent site that reviews freeware computer programs and there is a newsletter with reviews, tips and tricks. http://freewarewiki.com/

Internet Tutorials. How to choose the best search engine for your needs. http://www.internettutorials.net/choose.html

Jobcentre Plus. This is a government site where you might find work. http://www.jobcentreplus.gov.uk/JCP/

JustJobs4Students. As the name suggests, it's aimed directly at you and you could find a job here. http:\\www.justjobs4students.co.uk

Student Loan Company (SLC). Currently this supplies the cheapest loans available for students. http://www.slc.co.uk/

Surfwax. A meta-search engine. To see more about your search results click on "Full Text of Results". http://www.surfwax.com

Synonym.com. This is an online site that suggests a word of similar meaning which can be useful when you are trying to avoid using the same word in close proximity. http://www.synonym.com/ See also the thesaurus section of http://dictionary.reference.com/

The Internet Public Library. An excellent way in to information on different subjects – you can follow your own nose on this one. http://www.ipl.org/div/subject/

Wikepedia. An online encyclopaedia that people (including you) can add to if they wish. It's worth looking at, is often a good place to start with, but be cautious in citing it, as in the past the information has not always been 100 per cent correct. http://www.wikepedia.org/

Reminder: the Internet alters regularly and some of these references will get out of date. You may have to search for them using your Internet browser, or Google them as we currently say, and some will doubtless disappear. New good sites will continue to emerge. This list will eventually appear ludicrously old fashioned and be a source of embarrassment to me.

Appendix B. Favourite free computer programs

To obtain any of these programs that I personally like and use, search the Internet using your web browser for the program name plus "download". If any programs have gone commercial by the time you read this and a freeware version is no longer supplied, there is a site that has the last available free version of many programs – it's worth checking out for the one you seek at http://www.321download.com/LastFreeware/

40tude Dialog	A good dedicated newsreader.
Ad-Aware SE Personal	Helps keep spyware off your computer.
AVG Anti-Virus	Updated very regularly and works well for me.
Cobian Backup	Excellent back-up program for your important files.
Copernic Agent	A meta-search engine for use on the Internet; the Basic version is free.
Copernic Desktop Search	Lets you locate text on your own computer to find the old file you need.
CutePDF Writer	Turns word processor documents into PDF files.
DVD Decrypter	Removes protection from your DVDs to allow you to copy them as a back-up.
DVD Shrink	Allows you to shrink large DVDs to copy onto one disc.

EasyCleaner	Cleans up your registry, finds and get rids of duplicate files, and more.
Faststone Capture	Allows you to copy and save a part or all of any window as an image.
Faststone Image Viewer	See all the pictures on your computer and tinker with them at will.
Firefox	A great web browser with tabs, pop-up blocker and more.
First Page 2006	An excellent free webpage design program. I currently prefer it to NVU.
FreeUndelete	When you've deleted a file, emptied the Recycle Bin, then want the file back, this program should do it.
Gimp	Image manipulation: change dpi, alter size, save in a different format and more.
Handy Recovery	Another good file recovery program.
Mailwasher	Check out your emails on the server and help keep spam/viruses off your machine.
NVU	Build your own webpage with this.
OpenOffice	A good all-round office suite – save as RTF for maximum compatibility; includes free PDF maker.
Restoration	Another good file recovery program program.
Roboform	Lets you fill in forms online with your saved information *and* can protect your passwords, even generating them.
Safarp Uninstaller	Quickly un-install or repair programs.
SmartFTP	Allows file transfer across the Internet.
Snadboys Revelation	Reveals an asterisked password on your machine if you have forgotten what the darn thing was.

Spell.exe	Puts a spell-checker into Outlook Express for those who do not have Word or another Microsoft program.
Spybot	Helps keep spyware off your computer.
SpywareBlaster	Helps keep spyware off your computer.
Zone Alarm	An old and trusty firewall to keep you hidden online and help prevent your machine being taken over by outsiders.

Reminder: the Internet alters regularly and you can guarantee that some of these programs will eventually cease to be available and new good programs will appear.

Index

A

abbreviations, 64, 65, 102, 114
approaching assignments, 77, 79, 81, 82, 84, 85
assembling reports, 133, 134, 135
assessment, 27, 120, 123, 135

B

body language, 91, 94, 95
book lists, 51, 164, 168
brainstorming, 83, 116, 131, 132, 134

C

cheating, 124, 127
choosing where to live, 10, 13, 14, 162
clubs and societies, 6, 7, 23, 24
computers, 39, 40, 41, 51, 54, 55, 56, 60, 76, 101, 104, 108, 109, 111, 114, 121, 133, 134, 144, 146, 169, 171
CV, your, 19, 49, 130, 134, 142, 163, 168

D

daily list, 8-10
diary, 8, 10, 110, 117

E

essay length, 85, 90
essay tips, 102-108
essay tips – do!, 107
essay tips – don't!, 102
exam kit, 117, 125, 127
examinations, 115, 116, 117, 118, 119, 120, 123, 124, 125, 126, 127
eye contact, 90, 97, 99, 148, 154, 157

F

failing an assignment, 111, 112, 113
filing notes, 30, 63, 75, 76
finances, 10, 16, 17, 18
food and cooking, 10, 11, 12, 14-16
freedom, 1, 4, 8, 23, 24, 33, 41, 42, 164
fresher week, 7, 16, 17, 21, 22, 162, 164

G

goals of a university, 25
good words and phrases to use, 151
group projects, *and see* team skill, 50, 131, 132, 133, 134, 135, 137, 139

H

handouts, 28, 61, 62, 90, 94, 95, 97, 99, 144, 147, 154, 155, 157
home, returning, 159-60

175

housing, 10-12, 24, 161, 162, 165, 167, 168

I

Internet, 18, 39, 41, 49, 56, 57, 58, 60, 80, 84, 86, 124, 144, 169, 170, 171, 173

J

jobs, 2, 3, 4, 16, 17, 19, 23, 36, 39, 41, 49, 58, 63, 69, 85, 111, 129, 130, 137, 138, 142, 160, 163, 165, 168, 169

L

lab work, 9, 28, 29, 30, 70
learning tips, 29, 30, 37, 38, 39, 43, 44, 46, 47, 48, 49, 50, 60, 61, 62, 138
lectures, 1, 8, 9, 27, 28, 30, 37, 38, 44, 48, 50, 52, 53, 61-68, 71, 73, 79
library, 21, 22, 26, 28, 36, 38, 41, 47, 51, 52, 55-57, 60, 66, 68, 80, 86, 116, 164, 170
living cheaply, 19, 20

M

marketable skills, *see:* transferable skills
marking systems, 109, 110
mature students, 17, 34-38, 40, 42, 131, 151
motivation, 2, 8, 10, 23, 24, 35, 39, 42, 43, 58, 61, 63, 79, 91, 160, 161
multiple-choice, 29, 120-123, 124, 127

N

negative phrases to avoid, 152, 153
nerves *and see:* stress, relaxation techniques, 91, 98

O

oral presentations, 27, 28, 34, 85, 89, 91, 94-97, 98, 99, 102, 146, 166
outline, 69, 90, 119, 124, 131, 132, 134, 139, 147
outline, course, 61, 73
outline, lecture, 62, 63
outline, skeleton, 46, 47, 48, 50, 60, 77, 79, 83, 84, 86, 101, 103, 104, 107, 111, 115, 117, 118, 119
outlines, 117, 134
overhead transparencies, 63, 90, 94, 146-148, 150, 154, 155, 157

P

pattern method of note-taking, 65, 67, 83
personal problems, 31, 33
plagiarism, 50, 85
plans and planning, 47, 60, 77, 79, 108, 112, 116, 118, 119, 125, 126, 127, 147, 151
props, using in presentations, 142, 143, 149, 154, 155, 157

Q

questions, dealing with, 22, 81, 89, 95, 97, 99, 118, 121, 122, 123, 125, 126, 127, 135, 153, 157, 159, 163

R

reading efficiently, 53, 54, 55
reading lists, *and see* book lists, 21
reasons for going to university, 2-4, 23
relaxation techniques, 9, 33, 45, 47, 91-94, 98, 99, 116, 117
reliability of data, 84

resources, using, 55, 57, 60
returning home, problems, 159-160
role-playing, 28, 29, 95, 141, 142, 144, 145, 150, 152, 153, 154, 155, 157, 163, 165

S

second year, preparation, 161-165
seminars, 1, 9, 28, 29, 49, 69, 79, 154
sexism, 105, 112, 114
sexual harassment, 32
skeleton outline, *see* outline, skeleton
skills, 3, 23, 27, 35, 46, 55, 69, 85, 86, 94, 129, 135, 137, 141, 161, 163, 166, 167
small group working, 29, 49, 131-133, 134, 135, 136, 137, 138, 139, 150
social life and partying, 6, 13, 23, 164
socialising, 22, 24, 164, 166
special issues for mature students, 17, 34-38, 40, 42, 151
speech habits, poor, 95-97, 98, 99, 146, 149
speed reading, 54
SQ3R, the approach of, 53-54, 55, 60
starting assignments, 77-79, 110
stress, 33, 70, 91, 94, 98, 116, 120
study-buddy, 30-31, 37, 39, 44, 48, 49, 51, 58, 59, 60, 62, 66, 68, 69, 79, 83, 91, 104, 107, 111, 116, 127, 137, 166

study-group, 30, 31, 39, 42, 48-50, 51, 52, 58, 60, 66, 83, 86, 131, 138, 166

T

taking notes, 2, 27, 28, 37, 43, 44, 45, 46, 51, 52, 54, 62, 63-66, 68, 69, 70, 73, 75, 76
taping lectures, 66-68
team skills, 129-130
textbooks, 22, 28, 36, 37, 43, 46, 47, 48, 49, 50-52, 54, 55, 60, 62, 64, 66, 69, 79, 111, 115, 116, 121, 164
timetable, 8, 9, 10, 23, 39, 51, 110, 131, 139, 143, 160
transferable skills, 3, 49, 58, 69, 87, 89, 124, 130, 136, 137, 138, 139, 141, 142, 155, 157, 163, 168
transport, 10, 11, 12, 13-14, 21, 24, 117, 167
true–false tests, 120, 123, 127
tutorials, 1, 8, 9, 27, 28-29, 30, 58, 69, 71, 72, 73, 79, 142

U

university is different, 4

V

visual aids, 146-149
voice, using well, 91, 96-97, 98, 99, 145, 149, 150, 155
voice-recognition software, 76

W

weekly schedule, 8, 31, 39, 51, 110
what's in it for me?, 3, 142, 152
workshops, 1, 8, 9, 28, 29, 30, 70, 71, 73, 79
write-in answers, 120, 122, 123, 127

177

writing problems, 64, 71, 86,
    101, 102-108, 111, 114, 120,
    125, 127, 156
writing style, 108

Printed in the United Kingdom
by Lightning Source UK Ltd.
131599UK00001B/107/A